"Darrell Bock is one of the church's finest New Testament scholars. He has the unique ability to write on both the technical and popular levels and presents a biblical theology of the gospel that is clear, robust, and holistic. This is a valuable contribution to helping us rightly understand the greatness of the gospel."

—**Daniel L. Akin**, president, Southeastern
Baptist Theological Seminary

"Darrell Bock has written a fine biblical theology of the gospel based on his wide studies in the Gospels and Acts. He shows that the gospel has a transformative power to bring a knowledge of God, a knowledge of self, a new way of living, and membership in a new family. The love of God revealed in Jesus' death and resurrection binds us to Him, generates our love, and motivates our service. Bock's study expands our view of the gospel and corrects faulty common 'gospels' in our world today. Highly recommended!"

—**Ed Blum**, general editor, Holman Christian Standard Bible

"Bock teaches us the essence of the best news ever told. The gospel is so much more than good advice . . . it is the message of life, hope, grace, and Jesus Himself! Get ready to be reminded why it is the *best news ever!*"

—**Pete Briscoe**, senior pastor, Bent Tree Bible Fellowship
Dallas, Texas

"One of today's most prominent theologians takes a fresh look at the old, old story—the gospel. This is not a book just for your shelf; it is a must read for every pastor for both doctrinal study and practical application."

—**Mac Brunson**, senior pastor, First Baptist Church
Jacksonville, Florida

"*Recovering the Real Lost Gospel* is a welcomed corrective and timely guide for so many individuals and churches who seemingly have lost their way amidst the confusing spirituality and mixed religious messages of our day."

—**David S. Dockery**, president, Union University

"You are holding in your hands a really rare book—one that goes all the way back to the New Testament in connecting the gospel and the cross with the life of discipleship and the mission of the church in a broken world that needs the message of grace. Darrell Bock is one of our best biblical theologians and is at his best in this new study."

—**Timothy George**, dean, Beeson Divinity School, Samford University

"Darrell Bock has done for us what is necessary for any genuine reconsideration of the meaning of 'gospel' by walking us through the core New Testament teachings again. All vacuous and theoretical discussions of 'gospel' fade away when we return to the wellspring."

—**Mel Lawrenz**, Minister at Large, Elmbrook Church
Brookfield, Wisconsin

"Too many Christians think of 'the gospel' as merely the last page of an evangelistic tract. Bock demonstrates with clarity and vision that the gospel is better news than some have dared to hope. Read this book, and let its wisdom drive you to worship and to mission."

—**Russell D. Moore**, dean, School of Theology,
The Southern Baptist Theological Seminary

"Bock has delivered the gospel message in a new way, skillfully weaving passages and themes into a theological rope that at the same time feels very comfortable and immensely strong!"

—**Doug Pennoyer**, dean, Cook School of Intercultural Studies,
Biola University

"Is the gospel—the 'good news' that Jesus preached—the offer of forgiveness of sins, eternal life, prosperity, political power, social justice, religious power, or what? There is no more foundational issue for understanding God's purposes for Christians individually and for the church. Yet the church today has often clouded Jesus' gospel message. As a leading New Testament scholar, Darrell Bock uniquely and winsomely roots this gospel in the wide sweep of biblical revelation and challenges our conceptions of this most central message of Jesus by explaining carefully and fully the nature of the gospel as the fullness of life in the Spirit for everyday Christians."

—**Michael J. Wilkins**, distinguished professor of
New Testament Language and Literature and dean,
Talbot School of Theology, Biola University

RECOVERING THE

# REAL LOST

# GOSPEL

RECLAIMING
*THE GOSPEL*
AS GOOD NEWS

Darrell L. Bock

NASHVILLE, TENNESSEE

ISBN: 978-0-8054-6465-8

Published by B&H Publishing Group
Nashville, Tennessee

Dewey Decimal Classification: 226
Subject Heading: BIBLE. NEW TESTAMENT—STUDY \ BIBLE. N.T.
GOSPELS

Printed in the United States of America

2 3 4 5 6 7 8 9 10 11 12 • 17 16 15 14 13 12 11
VP

# Contents

# Foreword

This is a landmark book. It shares life-changing truth without wasting any words. Combining deep conviction with straightforward clarity, Darrell Bock shows how the full promise of the gospel—the wonderful good news of grace—is so often misunderstood, misapplied, and even missed because we don't know the whole story.

By tracing God's longsuffering love story of salvation from the beginning of the Bible to the end, Darrell demonstrates that the real gospel encompasses far more than just a transaction for sin, or a therapy for self, or a transportation to heaven. The gospel is transforming! It transforms everything about us, in us, around us, and for us. It does what we could never do for ourselves.

Reading this book will cause you to overflow with joy and gratitude for all that God has done for us through Jesus Christ. How could you not love a God who has done all this for you in His grace?

Enjoy this book; then pass it on to another.

Rick Warren
Saddleback Church
Lake Forest, CA

Introduction

# The Gospel from the Hub to the Whole: More Than Dying for Sin

• • • • • • • • • •

There are few things as precious to the Jesus Movement as the gospel. The word *gospel* means "good news." It is the sermon of the Jesus Movement. Its central proclamation is the good news of God's love and initiative not only to save us from hell, but also to bring us into a healthy relationship with Himself. The point of this book is that the gospel *is* good news, and its core is a restored relationship with God. I have shared this message since I became a Christian in college at the University of Texas. It stood at the core of my first ministry as a Young Life leader at Austin High School. It stands at the center of the church's mission in the world. If we ask what message Jesus brought, the short answer is simply this: He brought the good news that God's promised rule of deliverance had arrived. To experience the kingdom Jesus preached is to experience God's presence. Jesus died so His work could clear the way for a fresh work of God's grace (Titus 2:11–14).[1] That is good news indeed.

---

[1] Titus 2:11–14 states, "For the grace of God has appeared, with salvation for all people, instructing us to deny godlessness and worldly lusts and to live in a sensible, righteous, and godly way in the present age, while we wait for the blessed hope and the appearing of the glory of our great God and Savior, Jesus Christ. He gave Himself for us to redeem us from all lawlessness and to cleanse for Himself a special people, eager to do good works."

1

Yet when I hear some people preach the gospel today, I am not sure I hear its presentation as good news. Sometimes, I hear a therapeutic call—that God will make us feel better or prosper more. Other times, I hear so much about Jesus paying for sin that the gospel seems limited to a transaction—the removal of a debt. Or perhaps I hear it as a kind of spiritual root canal. Still other times, I hear a presentation that makes the gospel seem more about avoiding something from God versus experiencing something with Him. Other presentations make me think Jesus came to change politics in the world. Such political presentations make me wonder why God did not send Jesus to Rome rather than Jerusalem. None of these is the gospel I see in the Scripture, though some are closer than others.

This book is written with the conviction that the church has become cloudy on the purpose of gospel. I offer here a biblical theology of the gospel, something I do not think has been done in this way. I trace the key themes associated with the gospel's storyline. My intent is to present the key texts and discuss them to answer the question, *What does the Bible say about the gospel?* The goal is to rediscover the gospel as good news, something that can be lost on the church today.

If the church is in a fog on the gospel, then the church very much risks losing its reason for being. A misdirected gospel message robs the church of valuable momentum in the world. Nothing leads to stagnation more quickly than for an institution to forget why it exists. A plethora of messages from the church might lead to no message from the church. In sum, in many locales the gospel has gone missing, and wherever that takes place, the church suffers, God's people lose their way, and the world lacks what it so desperately needs—an experience of God's presence. Worse than that, people coming into the church lose sight of why they really are there and what it is they should be doing for God. An unclear gospel means trying to get somewhere unknown without a map; there's a good chance you won't get where you're supposed to go.

I wish to take a close look at the gospel as the New Testament presents it. We will look for its key features, highlighting key attributes tied to it as we go. We also will pay attention to the tone that accompanies the message, asking if the way we present the gospel is as important as what we say about it. This book involves a mission of rediscovery, reclaiming a message that has much to offer individuals and a needy world. A church that knows what its good news is and how to share it has a chance of being good news for a spiritually needy world that often gropes after God but struggles to find Him.

## The Starting Point but Not the Whole Message: The Cross

A key premise of our study is that the cross is the hub of the gospel, but Jesus' dying for sin is *not* the entire gospel. In fact, only to speak of Jesus dying for sin—even to speak of Jesus dying for sin *and* rising again—is to give only about half of the gospel message. We preach the cross because it is at the core of the gospel. It makes discussing and presenting the gospel fairly straightforward. By doing so we echo Paul, who used the image of the cross in Corinthians to summarize and highlight his view of the gospel message.

In 1 Cor 1:23, Paul says that he preaches "Christ crucified, a stumbling block to the Jews and foolishness to the Greeks." For some, this text and many others like it in Paul's writings show that the cross is the gospel. For example, Paul in 1 Cor 15:3–5 summarizes the gospel as the fact that Jesus "died for our sins according to the Scriptures, that He was buried, that He was raised on the third day according to the Scriptures, and that he appeared to Cephas." Once again, the cross is at the core of the gospel message. How can we suggest that the cross is not all there is to the gospel when Paul uses it, seemingly, as his summation?

When Paul refers to the cross in this early part of 1 Corinthians, the term *cross* functions as a hub and a synecdoche for all that Jesus' work brings. A synecdoche is a part that represents the whole. I mention one central thing to picture all of it. For example, if I speak of the Law and the Prophets, I am speaking of the whole Old Testament. If I speak of fifty head of cattle, I'm talking about fifty whole cows—heads, hooves, bodies, and tails—not just fifty heads. Likewise, when Paul speaks of the cross here, he is using the word as a synecdoche for the whole of the gospel. But the death of Jesus is not the whole of the gospel any more than a head is the whole of a cow. It is vitally important, yes. The gospel could not live without the cross any more than a cow could live without a head. But still, the events of the first Easter weekend are not the whole story.

First Corinthians 1:30 says as much when it speaks of how being in Jesus Christ (the product of benefiting from the gospel) means access to God's wisdom, righteousness, sanctification, and redemption.[2] In 2:2, to know Jesus, the One who was crucified, is to know Him at all of these levels.[3]

Why is this distinction so important? That is what this book is about. Most gospel presentations I hear focus often exclusively on the cross. The gospel is set forth primarily, if not exclusively, as a transaction to be experienced in a moment in time. To believe, or to exercise faith, is to trigger the transaction and fulfill the gospel. Now what makes this tricky is that there *is* a transaction that is a part of the gospel and that allows us to experience God's good news; however, there is more to this gospel, as the Pauline cross texts suggest.

The danger in seeing or preaching the gospel only as a transaction is that once the "deal" is done, the believer may have the sense that he or she has checked the box and is done with the gospel having procured the salvation and avoided hell. But as I hope to show in the subsequent chapters, this actually only represents the starting point for God's good news.

Is there a way to affirm Jesus' death for sin as a key element of the gospel and yet not lose a comprehensive appreciation for all that the gospel is? My hope is that by working through the elements of what is associated with the gospel, we will recover what is often lost as good news, not only in preaching about the gospel,

---

[2] First Corinthians 1:30 says, "But from Him you are in Christ Jesus, who for us became wisdom from God, as well as righteousness, sanctification, and redemption."

[3] First Corinthians 2:2 says, "For I determined to know nothing among you except Jesus Christ and Him crucified."

but also from what results in response to it. The gospel starts with a promise: a relationship in the Spirit. It is pictured as a meal and a washing: the Lord's Table and baptism. It is rooted in a unique action supplying a unique need: the cross. It is inaugurated as a gift that is the sign of the arrival of the new era: Pentecost. It is affirmed in divine action and Scripture: God working uniquely and inseparably through Jesus. It is embraced in a turn that ends in faith: invoking the name of Jesus. It involves a different kind of power and is designed to be a way of life: reconciliation and the power of God unto salvation. My prayer is that a look at these themes will open up a renewed understanding of how the gospel of the kingdom works, setting up the kind of faith and walk God desires from His people. Once we appreciate all God has done for us through the gospel, we are in a better position to love and serve God and His gospel more faithfully. And so we begin with the promise that stands at the opening of our survey, namely, how John the Baptist prepared the way for us as he introduced Jesus and why He came.

## Questions for Discussion

1. What is the problem of not presenting the gospel clearly?
2. Is the cross all the gospel? Why or why not? How does the cross function in the gospel?
3. What is 1 Corinthians 15 trying to say? What does it not cover?
4. What is involved in the gospel beyond the cross?
5. What difference does this theme make for me personally?

# Chapter 1

# The Gospel Starts
# with a Promise:
# Relationship in the Spirit

· · · · · · · · · ·

J ust for a moment, forget about sin. Forget about the debt
we owe and the prospect of God's punishment. Those are
all important things to consider, and we will consider them
soon enough. But for the moment, I want to focus on something else: instead of sin, I want to think about the deep needs
that define our humanity. To be human is to be aware that we
yearn for things that we just can't get on our own, whatever our
culture of self-sufficiency might tell us. We desire to be connected to something outside ourselves. We long to know why
we exist at all. These needs and longings are central to the
Bible's story. The gospel starts with a promise that addresses
the deepest of human needs. Where relationships are broken,
the gospel brings restoration.

## The Covenants: God's Plan to Restore Relationships

### The Abrahamic Covenant

The gospel didn't begin in Matthew 1:1. It began many centuries
earlier in the dusty regions of the Middle East. God made a promise to Abraham, an old man who would give rise to a special
people. In the midst of a world that had ignored its Creator for the
elevation of their own glory (Gen 11), God moved to deliver
humanity from its own foibles. In Genesis 12:1–3, God made a
commitment with Abraham:

The LORD said to Abram:
Go out from your land,
your relatives,
and your father's house
to the land that I will show you.
I will make you into a great nation,
I will bless you,
I will make your name great,
and you will be a blessing.
I will bless those who bless you,
I will curse those who treat you with contempt,
and all the peoples on earth
will be blessed through you.

That commitment became known as the Abrahamic covenant. Perhaps the greatest of God's promises to Abraham was this: through Abraham, God's blessing would penetrate throughout the world. In that first declaration of the promise, God offered no details as to how this blessing would spread. That story would develop across several centuries and inspired writers. In that unfolding story is our story—our need for promise and the hope of restoration.

The context of this initial promise is important. In Genesis 1–11 we see how humanity had gone its own way, consistently going astray from the Creator. Whether we think of the individual acts of Adam or Cain or turn to the corporate actions before the flood or in building the tower of Babel, people showed a consistent tendency, one they still have, to turn away God and toward their own interests. In many ways, the story of the Bible is the story of God's stubborn faithfulness to His creation and those He had made in His own image—His commitment to pursue them in steadfast love and patience. God's love is the core of the gospel. The needs of humanity have run deep for a long time.

God's promise to Abraham grew. Part of the original promise was that Abraham would father a special seed (Gen 12:2), a people in touch with the true God. That story—the story of Israel's origins—is told from Genesis through Deuteronomy (Gen 13:13–17).[1] Abraham did father a seed in the figures of Isaac, Jacob, and the twelve sons who followed Jacob, known as the patriarchs. From them emerged the nation known as Israel. God's program was revealed to this people. They were the bearers of God's promise and revelation. They experienced a deliverance through Moses, pictured in a God who kept an ear open to people. They became a nation called to honor God (Exod 19:3–6).[2]

### The Davidic Covenant

Israel, however, had her own hopes, and they didn't always line up with God's hopes for her. She longed for a king like the other nations had; God was not good enough for them. God noted that the Israelites' request for a king was really a rejection of Him (1 Sam 8:6–7); nevertheless, He graciously granted their desire and through this eventually extended the promise He had made to Abraham.[3] This extended promise, known as the Davidic covenant, was a line of kings from the house of David (2 Sam 7:8–16):

> "Now this is what you are to say to My servant David:
> 'This is what the LORD of Hosts says: I took you from the pasture and from following the sheep to be ruler over My people Israel. I have been with you wherever you have gone, and I have destroyed all your enemies before you. I will make a name for you

---

[1] Genesis 13:13–17 says, "Now the men of Sodom were evil, sinning greatly against the LORD. After Lot had separated from him, the LORD said to Abram, 'Look from the place where you are. Look north and south, east and west, for I will give you and your offspring forever all the land that you see. I will make your offspring like the dust of the earth, so that if one could count the dust of the earth, then your offspring could be counted. Get up and walk from one end of the land to the other, for I will give it to you.'"

[2] Exodus 19:3–6 says, "Moses went up the mountain to God, and the LORD called to him from the mountain: 'This is what you must say to the house of Jacob, and explain to the Israelites: "You have seen what I did to the Egyptians and how I carried you on eagles' wings and brought you to Me. Now if you will listen to Me and carefully keep My covenant, you will be My own possession out of all the peoples, although all the earth is Mine, and you will be My kingdom of priests and My holy nation." These are the words that you are to say to the Israelites.'"

[3] First Samuel 8:6–7 says, "When they said, 'Give us a king to judge us,' Samuel considered their demand sinful, so he prayed to the LORD. But the LORD told him, 'Listen to the people and everything they say to you. They have not rejected you; they have rejected Me as their king.'"

like that of the greatest in the land. I will establish a place for My people Israel and plant them, so that they may live there and not be disturbed again. . . .

'When your time comes and you rest with your fathers, I will raise up after you your descendant, who will come from your body, and I will establish his kingdom. He will build a house for My name, and I will establish the throne of his kingdom forever. I will be a father to him, and he will be a son to Me. When he does wrong, I will discipline him with a human rod and with blows from others. But My faithful love will never leave him as I removed it from Saul; I removed him from your way. Your house and kingdom will endure before Me forever, and your throne will be established forever.'"

This regal line had a special relationship to God as His representative. The king of this dynasty was a son to God and God was his father (v. 14). Out of this promise came the hope for a unique king who would be the kind of ruler God desired. Out of this promise came the hope of a Messiah, a king who would bring peace and establish righteousness in line with promises God made originally to Abraham.

## *The New Covenant*
The majority of Israel's kings failed. They did not live up to God's ideals, reflecting instead the pattern of rebellion we have seen already. More often than not, they went their own way. Eventually God judged the nation, scattering them through war and exile. It was in this context that God promised a new covenant: a commitment to write His righteousness on the hearts of people and to fix them from the inside out with His very own presence and power. That commitment was revealed through Jeremiah (Jer 31:31–34):

"Look, the days are coming"—this is the LORD's declaration—
"when I will make a new covenant with the house of Israel and with the house of Judah. This one will not be like the covenant I made with their ancestors when I took them by the hand to bring them out of the land of Egypt—a covenant they broke even though I had married them"—the LORD's declaration. "Instead, this is the covenant I will make with the house of Israel after those days"—the LORD's declaration. "I will place My law

within them and write it on their hearts. I will be their God, and they will be My people. No longer will one teach his neighbor or his brother, saying: Know the LORD, for they will all know Me, from the least to the greatest of them"—the LORD's declaration. "For I will forgive their wrongdoing and never again remember their sin."

Two key ingredients came with this elaboration of God's promise. First, there would be forgiveness of sin; second, God's law would be written on the heart. That long history of unfaithfulness—even by God's own people—demonstrated that human beings didn't have it within themselves to keep their end of the covenant bargain. They needed God's presence and power within them.

Forgiveness never stood alone; it was designed to provide the way to a restored relationship with God. Consider what God said through Ezekiel:

I will also sprinkle clean water on you, and you will be clean. I will cleanse you from all your impurities and all your idols. I will give you a new heart and put a new spirit within you; I will remove your heart of stone and give you a heart of flesh. I will place My Spirit within you and cause you to follow My statutes and carefully observe My ordinances. (Ezek 36:25–27)

A new heart. A new Spirit. A new start. If God's people are going to obey God's law consistently, it won't be by trying harder. It will be by God's Spirit dwelling within them.

*Summary*

This overview of the promise of the Old Testament shows that behind the gospel stands the promise of three covenants that actually form a singular promise of God to fashion a people who themselves are a reflection of God's promise and blessing living in a world filled with need. Together the Abrahamic, Davidic, and New covenants form the gospel's backbone. God would form a people through whom the world would be blessed. He would do it through a promised king, a Messiah. That king would bring two key things the world desperately needed: forgiveness and a restored relationship with the living God. The two were always connected to be good news from God.

## The Proclamation: From John the Baptist to Jesus

*Luke 3:16*

Tucked away in Luke's Gospel is a passage most of us pass by very quickly, yet in it are some of the most profound things said in the entire Bible. It's too bad Luke 3:16 is not as well known in the church as John 3:16. The promise and revelation in Luke 3:16 literally run through all of Luke and Acts.[4] In this verse, John the Baptist says, "I baptize you with water, but One is coming who is more powerful than I. I am not worthy to untie the strap of His sandals. He will baptize you with the Holy Spirit and fire."

John made this remark in response to speculation that he might be the Christ. What is the sign of the new era? God's giving of His Spirit to His people—not the outward, physical sign of water baptism, but the inward sign of a Spirit baptism. This new era will come in the person of the One who follows John: Jesus Himself. In bringing the Spirit, Jesus will bring a renewed relationship. Remember what Ezekiel said? "I will give you a new heart and put a new spirit within you." According to John the Baptist, Jesus was coming to fulfill that promise.

But there is more to this verse. It is found in the remark that John was not worthy to unstrap the sandal of the One to Come. Two points help us to appreciate what John is affirming. First, John says this as a prophet of God. In the vocational ladder of jobs God can give, few rank higher than prophet. In fact, later Jesus called John the greatest born of woman (Luke 7:28).[5] So this is not just anyone saying he is unworthy to serve the One to Come—it is a prophet of God, the greatest of the prophets at that.

---

[4] Luke wrote both the Gospel of Luke and the book of Acts, which picks up where the Gospels leave off. I speak of Luke–Acts because these two books are essentially volume 1 and volume 2 of Luke's account of the beginnings of the Church.

[5] Luke 7:28 says, "I tell you, among those born of women no one is greater than John, but the least in the kingdom of God is greater than he."

Second, let us consider John's saying that he is not worthy to untie the strap of his master's sandal. In Judaism, a person was not to become a slave. However, if he did, there was one thing later Jewish tradition noted a Hebrew slave should never do: he should never untie the strap of his master's sandal in order to wash his feet (*Mekilta de Rabbi Ishmael Nezikin 1* on Exod 21:2).[6] Unstrapping a master's sandal was seen as too demeaning for a Hebrew to perform.

The difference between John as a prophet and the person of the One to Come is so great that John, even though he is a prophet, is not worthy to perform even the most demeaning task of a slave. The One to Come is that unique. The significance of this point cannot be overstated. The Messiah to come is a figure of a different order. The chasm between Him and a prophet is vast. The One who brings God's promise is not merely another in a line of prophets but someone in a completely different, utterly unique category.

I love to make this point for those who tend to see Jesus as just another religious great. That is not how the person who pointed to Him saw it at all. The difference between them was too great for them to be seen in the same light.

I used this passage once in India to explain to a Hindi audience just how unique the Promised One is. My point was that John the Baptist was a figure whose activity was predicted in the Bible centuries before he ministered (Isa 40:3–5).[7] Not too many of us have our career outlined for us in advance! Yet despite John's high position in God's plan and program, the role of the One to Come was even more elevated. Even as a prophet, John would have been

---

[6] Jacob Lauterbach, *Mekilta de-Rabbi Ishmael* (1933; repr., Philadelphia: Jewish Publication Society, 2004), 2:358. The remark appears in a section discussing the six years a slave can serve. He should not wash the feet of his master, put shoes on him, carry things for him to a bathhouse, lift him by the hips as he goes upstairs, or carry him in a chair or sedan chair.

[7] Isaiah 40:3–5 says, "A voice of one crying out: Prepare the way of the LORD in the wilderness; make a straight highway for our God in the desert. Every valley will be lifted up, and every mountain and hill will be leveled; the uneven ground will become smooth, and the rough places a plain. And the glory of the LORD will appear, and all humanity will see it together, for the mouth of the LORD has spoken."

honored to have done a most demeaning task for Him and felt unworthy to perform such a task. The bottom line of the new era's arrival is the coming of the Spirit. That is the provision that shows the promise of God has come. The goal of all of this covenant activity is to restore a lost relationship—to connect God and His people from within. Once the Promised One arrived, the focus turned to the hope of this restored relationship within the realized rule of God, what Scripture calls the kingdom of God. This idea of God's effective presence and direction within His people stood at the forefront of the gospel. The gospel is about the privilege of God entering our lives permanently from within our beings, restoring His relationship with us, and making us a part of His precious family. That was the good news John the Baptist pointed to in Luke 3:16, a verse as relevant to the gospel as John 3:16.

The importance of this idea becomes increasingly evident throughout the rest of Luke–Acts. The promise of renewed relationship and a divine presence within believers runs like a golden thread through these two New Testament books.

*Luke 24:49*
In Luke 24, Jesus has risen from the dead and appeared to the disciples. He told them the Law and the Prophets have predicted three things:

1. The Christ must suffer.
2. He must rise from the dead on the third day.
3. "Repentance for forgiveness of sins would be proclaimed in His name to all the nations" (see Luke 24:45–47).[8]

Our reading of the passage shouldn't stop there. In verse 49, Jesus says, "And look, I am sending you *what My Father promised.* As for you, stay in the city until you are empowered from on

---

[8] Luke 24:45–47 says, "Then He opened their minds to understand the Scriptures. He also said to them, 'This is what is written: the Messiah would suffer and rise from the dead the third day, and repentance for forgiveness of sins would be proclaimed in His name to all the nations, beginning at Jerusalem.'"

high." Jesus will provide what John the Baptist said the Messiah would provide: the Spirit of God. Through that Spirit, God shows His way to the people He is forming to be His own, and He *empowers* them to walk in the way.

*Acts 1:4–5*
If there is any doubt that Jesus is talking about the empowerment of the Holy Spirit, Acts 1 removes it. At the beginning of Acts, the disciples are gathered in Jerusalem awaiting their orders from the Father, as the risen Christ had commanded them to do.[9] In Acts 1:5, Jesus tells the disciples something that we have heard before: "For John baptized with water, but you will be baptized with the Holy Spirit not many days from now." Immediately, we can see the connection to Luke 3:16 and what John the Baptist had taught. The signal of the new era, the sign of God's presence, and the indwelling power of God are all wrapped up in the promise to provide the Spirit in the restored relationship the Messiah brings to those who are His.

*Acts 2*
But we still are not done with this theme in Luke–Acts. Peter's preaching in Acts 2 reaffirms and develops this idea even more. This is a key passage when discussing the gospel. In many ways, it is the first gospel message preached in Scripture, so it tells us much about what the earliest disciples emphasized in presenting the good news of God. And the disciples' emphasis, we will see, is on the promise of God's Spirit, the sign that God was forming a new people from the old in a fresh way.

Acts 2 describes the event that we often refer to as Pentecost. Pentecost was a Jewish feast day that, it seems, had come to be associated with the day the law had been given to Israel.[10] On this

---

[9] Acts 1:4 reads, "While He was together with them, He commanded them not to leave Jerusalem, but to wait for the Father's promise. 'This,' He said, 'is what you heard from Me. . . .'"

[10] It is possible the Jewish book of Jubilees sees Pentecost and the giving of the law as having fallen on the same day (A. Weiser, *EDNT* 3:70; BDAG 796; O. Betz, *TDNT* 9:296; Tob 2:1; 2 Macc 12:32).

particular Pentecost, just weeks after the resurrection of Jesus, a new salvation event was the topic of discussion: the arrival of God's promised Spirit and the arrival of the new era of God, both for the world and God's people.

That day the disciples were filled with the Holy Spirit and began "speaking of the mighty deeds of God" in all the languages of the people from many countries who were in Jerusalem that day. The people were amazed and wondered what it could mean, these uneducated fishermen and others from Galilee speaking in foreign tongues. Some of them theorized that the disciples must have been drunk!

The bulk of Acts 2 is devoted to a sermon in which Peter explains what was really happening. These people were not drunk, he explained. Rather, their actions were evidence that a long-cherished promise from the prophet Joel was being fulfilled:

> After this I will pour out My Spirit on all humanity; then your sons and your daughters will prophesy, your old men will have dreams, and your young men will see visions. I will even pour out My Spirit on the male and female slaves in those days. I will display wonders in the heavens and on the earth: blood, fire, and columns of smoke. The sun will be turned to darkness and the moon to blood before the great and awe-inspiring Day of the LORD comes. Then everyone who calls on the name of Yahweh will be saved, for there will be an escape for those on Mount Zion and in Jerusalem, as the LORD promised, among the survivors the LORD calls. (Joel 2:28–32)

This strange behavior by the disciples, Peter emphasized, was the work of the Spirit through those who had received the Spirit. Those in whom the Spirit dwells—like those disciples—had both a mission and the empowerment to share it with others.

Later in the sermon, Peter quotes Psalm 16, making the case that this passage, written hundreds of years earlier, referred to Jesus. "Thou wilt not abandon my soul to Hades," the psalm reads, "nor allow thy Holy One to undergo decay." As Peter noted, death was not able to hold Jesus just as the psalm had declared.

Next, Peter turns to the promise of the Father, first seen in Luke 3:16 and repeated in Luke 24:49 and Acts 1:4–5. Peter says in verses 32–33, "God has resurrected this Jesus. We are all witnesses of this. Therefore, since [Jesus] has been exalted to the right hand of God and has received from the Father the promised Holy Spirit, [Jesus] has poured out what you both see and hear." Here is the sign that the new era had arrived through the mediating work of the One at God's right hand, just as John the Baptist had said.

So a few verses later, Peter sums up the point: "Therefore let all the house of Israel know with certainty that God has made this Jesus, whom you crucified, both Lord and Messiah!" Peter then calls on his audience to respond and be baptized for the forgiveness of sins *and the reception of the Spirit of God, the reception of a promise God had made to enable His people.* Here is the offer as expressed in Acts 2:38–39: "'Repent,' Peter said to them, 'and be baptized, each of you, in the name of Jesus the Messiah for the forgiveness of your sins, and you will receive the gift of the Holy Spirit. For the promise is for you and for your children, and for all who are far off, as many as the Lord our God will call.'"

Thus, the first gospel message of the early church spoke of Jesus giving the Spirit in order to forge a fresh relationship between God and His people. This gospel message called people into a new affiliation with God that permitted them to pass from being subject to God's judgment into the new life the Spirit of God brings. It called them to experience a vibrancy of life that even life under God's law had not been able to provide. Here was good news: The way into relationship with God had been opened up in a fresh new way through Jesus.

Two thousand years of the church's telling the story can dull the sense of wonder the gospel should bring. Here is the Creator God reaching down to touch a rebellious people's heart through a sacrifice that He Himself brings, so that those He created may experience the life they were originally designed to live—a life in harmony with creation because it is in accord with the Creator. The gospel is not about a death but about a death that leads many into life. It is not about avoiding something but gaining someone precious, a new vibrant relationship with the gracious and self-sacrificing God who created us to know and follow Him.

*Acts 11:15–18*

Our journey through the gospel as promised is not done. The gospel is about more than saving the individual. It has a much larger corporately driven goal: the reconciliation of people to both God and one another. A hint of this comes in Luke 1:16–17, which describes John the Baptist's mission in preparing the way for the gospel: "He will turn many of the sons of Israel to the Lord their God. And he will go before Him in the spirit and power of Elijah, to turn the hearts of fathers to their children, and the disobedient to the understanding of the righteous, to make ready for the Lord a prepared people." John's message was not only to bring people back to God but also to bring them back to one another in healthy relationships that had gone stale.

The book of Acts also points to this element of reconciliation in the gospel. After Cornelius and his Gentile family had embraced the Lord, the Spirit came upon them even before Peter had finished his message to them. Some thought including Gentiles in the new community without making them live like Jews was a mistake and challenged Peter for welcoming these new believers into the community. Peter explains that God showed what was to be done by how He had responded. Acts 11:15–18 summarizes, "As I began to speak, the Holy Spirit came down on them, just as on us at the beginning. Then I remembered the word of the Lord, how He said, 'John baptized with water, but you will be baptized with the Holy Spirit.' Therefore, if God gave them the same gift that He also gave to us when we believed in the Lord Jesus Christ, how could I possibly hinder God?" When they heard this, they became silent. Then they glorified God, saying, "So God has granted repentance resulting in life to even the Gentiles!" Now both Jews and Gentiles, groups comprising all the world's people, had access to the new life. The gift of the Spirit, the sign of this new era, came with faith in Jesus. Peter's mind went back to the words of Jesus, noted in Acts 1:4–5 that themselves were an echo of the promise John the Baptist uttered in Luke 3:16. The gospel is about a promise that brings people back to God and to each other. In a world desperate for peace, that is good news.

*Acts 13:23–25*

The golden thread of promise in the gospel reappears in Acts 13. In this chapter, Paul is preaching at Pisidea Antioch in a locale that now is located in the middle of Turkey. He summarizes the history of Israel. He starts with Abraham, then goes on to the exodus with Moses, on to Joshua, on to the period of the Judges, on to Saul, and then on to David. From here, Paul leaps all the way from David to John the Baptist and Jesus. A thousand years of Israel's history means nothing. That history drives toward David and promises made to this significant king. Speaking of David and promises made to him, Paul says in Acts 13:23–25, "From this man's descendants, according to the promise, God brought the Savior, Jesus, to Israel. Before He came to public attention, John had previously proclaimed a baptism of repentance to all the people of Israel. Then as John was completing his life work, he said, 'Who do you think I am? I am not the One. But look! Someone is coming after me, and I am not worthy to untie the sandals on His feet.'"

Does Paul's allusion to the completion of the promise look familiar? The untying of the sandals is an allusion back to the Luke 3:16 passage and the promise that the Messiah brings God's Spirit to His people. Paul concludes the message with this word of exhortation: "Therefore, let it be known to you, brothers, that through this man forgiveness of sins is being proclaimed to you, and everyone who believes in Him is justified from everything, which you could not be justified from through the law of Moses" (Acts 13:38–39). Here Jesus brings forgiveness and justification, things the law could not generate. As we see throughout Luke–Acts, forgiveness isn't an end in itself. The point of forgiveness is to remove the barrier that stands between us and God so that He can give us His Spirit and bring us into His everlasting family.

*Acts 15:7–9*

Our final passage in the thread appears at the Jerusalem Council in Acts 15. Once again, Peter is defending the manner in which Gentiles have been brought into the community alongside Jews. Acts 15:7–9 reads, "After there had been much debate, Peter stood up and said to them: 'Brothers, you are aware that in the early days God made a choice among you, that by my mouth the Gentiles would hear the gospel message and believe. And God, who knows the heart, testified to them by giving the Holy Spirit, just as He also did to us. He made no distinction between us and them, cleansing their hearts by faith.'"

By now, the argument ought to be familiar. God took the initiative in the gospel, showing that Gentiles who genuinely responded received the same Spirit originally given at Pentecost. Their hearts were cleansed by faith so God could come and indwell them. If God is present in them without their keeping the law, then we should not ask them to do something God did not ask them to do.

## Summary: The Gospel Is about a Promise

The golden thread we have traced reflects the message at the center of the gospel. God has taken the initiative in Jesus Christ to bring us into relationship with Him. At the core of that good news stands a promise to form a new relationship *and* a new community. God was remaking a people He had previously formed around His law. That law had not led God's people into righteousness, not because the law was flawed, but because we were. For a relationship with God to function, a new work had to be done from within the depths of the human soul. So God offered the hope of a promise, the hope of His Spirit poured out in the last days, and the hope of a new responsiveness etched in His children's hearts.

To clear the path for that new heart, it had to be evident that sin was costly and that it was an obstacle between God and people. Sin was a debt that could be repaid only at a deep, deep cost: the cost of a life. God paid the cost Himself through His Son, the Messiah. The evidence that Jesus is the Messiah is indicated not just by an empty tomb and resurrection but also by the provision of the very promise that pointed to the new era, the gift of a new relationship in the Spirit. John the Baptist had pointed to this as the test of whether the Promised One had come. In the Spirit's presence, God not only drew near but also showed that the real gospel was about regaining fellowship with Him and joining the reconciled people He had been dying to create.

## Questions for Discussion

1. How does each covenant relate to the gospel? How do the covenants as a whole relate to the gospel?
2. In the passage sequence from Luke–Acts, what is being highlighted as the key to the Messiah's coming and the work He does?
3. Describe the difference between John the Baptist and the One to Come.
4. How is the gospel about a promise?
5. What difference does this theme make for me personally?

# Chapter 2

# The Gospel Is a Meal and a Washing: The Lord's Table and Baptism

* * * * * * * * *

The church has two means by which it illustrates participation in the gospel for its members: the Lord's Table and baptism. Each rite highlights a distinct element of the gospel and is significant because it has been repeated in the church regularly. Baptism focuses on the individual's response. The table shows how God formed a people through the gospel. By looking at how the gospel is portrayed through the rites of the church, we can gain more insight into what the gospel is.

## Last Supper–Lord's Table: From Death into New Life and Community

The context for the Lord's Table is the significance of table fellowship in the ancient world. Sharing the table and a meal were the most intimate things people could do in the ancient world. It was a sign of acceptance and an indicator of friendship and kinship.

### Exodus 12: Passover

Nothing points to this setting more powerfully than the background to the Lord's Supper, the celebration of Passover. God instituted this meal to recall God's act of protection and deliverance that led to the exodus, the corporate saving act that forged Israel into a functioning nation, mentioned in Exodus 12:

The LORD said to Moses and Aaron in the land of Egypt: "This month is to be the beginning of months for you; it is the first month of your year. Tell the whole community of Israel that on the tenth day of this month they must each select an animal of the flock according to their fathers' households, one animal per household. If the household is too small for a whole animal, that person and the neighbor nearest his house are to select one based on the combined number of people; you should apportion the animal according to what each person will eat. You must have an unblemished animal, a year-old male; you may take it from either the sheep or the goats. You are to keep it until the fourteenth day of this month; then the whole assembly of the community of Israel will slaughter the animals at twilight. They must take some of the blood and put it on the two doorposts and the lintel of the houses in which they eat them. They are to eat the meat that night; they should eat it, roasted over the fire along with unleavened bread and bitter herbs. Do not eat any of it raw or cooked in boiling water, but only roasted over fire—its head as well as its legs and inner organs. Do not let any of it remain until morning; you must burn up any part of it that does remain until morning. Here is how you must eat it: dressed for travel, your sandals on your feet, and your staff in your hand. You are to eat it in a hurry; it is the LORD's Passover.

"I will pass through the land of Egypt on that night and strike every firstborn male in the land of Egypt, both man and beast. I am the LORD; I will execute judgments against all the gods of Egypt. The blood on the houses where you are staying will be a distinguishing mark for you; when I see the blood, I will pass over you. No plague will be among you to destroy you when I strike the land of Egypt.

"This day is to be a memorial for you, and you must celebrate it as a festival to the LORD. You are to celebrate it throughout your generations as a permanent statute. You must eat unleavened bread for seven days. On the first day you must remove yeast from your houses. Whoever eats what is leavened from the first day through the seventh day must be cut off from Israel. You are to hold a sacred assembly on the first day and another sacred assembly on the seventh day. No work may be done on those days except for preparing what people need to eat—you may do only that." (vv. 1–16)

Several features stand out about this meal:

1. It is a corporate exercise. All of Israel is to perform it annually as a way of remembering together what God had done for them.
2. At the same time, families are involved so that it also shows the relationship and acceptance people have in community.
3. To participate in the meal is to affirm a person's association with and loyalty to the one God of Israel in contrast to the multiple gods of others. The blood on the doorways of the homes was a "distinguishing mark." The blood covered the family and showed their allegiance to God, something He honored by passing over that house as judgment moved through the land of Pharaoh.
4. The Passover was to be celebrated annually to remember what God had done in freeing and forging the Israelites into a people. This deliverance involved more than an individual and was to be celebrated as a multigenerational, multifamily event.

This event was for the community; a foreigner or hired hand could not participate, as Exodus 12:43–48 indicates, unless they embraced the covenant relationship this meal celebrated.[1] This was a family meal and a meal of covenant affirmation. To participate was to say a person belonged to God's people and to the God who stood at the head of this community.

It is this meal that is modeled in the Last Supper Jesus ate with His disciples. All the corporate, familial, and allegiance dimensions of the Passover also apply to the Lord's Table.

---

[1] Exodus 12:43–48 says, "The Lord said to Moses and Aaron, 'This is the statute of the Passover: no foreigner may eat it. But any slave a man has purchased may eat it, after you have circumcised him. A temporary resident or hired hand may not eat the Passover. It is to be eaten in one house. You may not take any of the meat outside the house, and you may not break any of its bones. The whole community of Israel must celebrate it. If a foreigner resides with you and wants to celebrate the Lord's Passover, every male in his household must be circumcised, and then he may participate; he will become like a native of the land. But no uncircumcised person may eat it. The same law will apply to both the native and the foreigner who resides among you.'"

*The Last Supper*

Mark portrays the Last Supper as a Passover meal. Mark 14:12 notes how the disciples went to prepare for the meal: "On the first day of Unleavened Bread, when they sacrifice the Passover lamb, His disciples asked Him, 'Where do You want us to go and prepare the Passover so You may eat it?'" (cf. Matt 26:17). Luke 22:8 says it this way: "Jesus sent Peter and John, saying, 'Go and prepare the Passover meal for us, so we can eat it.'" It is this connection that tells us we should see the Last Supper and Lord's Table as sharing in the Passover's same corporate emphases.

This meal is important for a number of reasons. First, Jesus shows His authority in taking this meal and totally reframing its imagery around His own coming death. Here is a commemoration of God's saving of Israel. It spanned centuries, from the exodus to that night before Jesus died. It was commanded by God in the Pentateuch. Yet Jesus was so bold as to totally reconfigure Israel's most sacred meal so that henceforth it would commemorate a second divine act of salvation: the death of Jesus that would establish a new relationship with God. Even as He turns to face His death, Jesus' actions point to His authority.

Second, the symbolism introduced by Jesus points to the core action that triggers the new way, namely, His coming death. This action explains why the cross is so precious to the church. Sometimes people complain about God insisting on a death to bring about salvation. I recently gave a lecture in which a question from the audience was whether we should consider Jesus' death to be a kind of suicide because He chose to go to the cross.[2] In my response I made two points. The first was that the "suicide" charge fails in part because the story does not end with Jesus' death but with what emerged from it, a resurrection pointing to new life. Next, I noted that part of the reason for the death was to make

---

[2] Mark 14:61b–62 says, "Again the high priest questioned Him, 'Are You the Messiah, the Son of the Blessed One?' 'I am,' said Jesus, 'and all of you will see the Son of Man seated at the right hand of the Power and coming with the clouds of heaven.'" Jesus knew that affi rming this claim and a direct divine vindication would lead to His death. So Jesus' answer here sets the stage for His death. He chose to go to the cross by saying this.

clear the truth that sin costs and costs dearly. When, in the bread and wine of the Last Supper, Jesus brought new imagery to the death that led to God's new saving act, He was purposely pointing to the reason such a death was necessary. It was "for the many."

Matthew 26:26 records Jesus' words over the bread: "As they were eating, Jesus took bread, blessed and broke it, gave it to the disciples, and said, 'Take and eat it; this is My body.'" Mark 14:22 reads, "As they were eating, He took bread, blessed and broke it, gave it to them, and said, 'Take it; this is My body.'" The association here is between bread, which sustains life, and Jesus' body. Luke 22:19 has a more liturgical feel to it as well as a little more explanation: "And He took bread, gave thanks, broke it, gave it to them, and said, 'This is My body, which is given for you. Do this in remembrance of Me.'" Here the body is given for others. What was implicit in Matthew and Mark is explicit in Luke. Paul makes it clear that from the earliest days, the Church did remember Jesus' breaking of the bread, passing it on explicitly as a piece of tradition: "For I received from the Lord what I also passed on to you: on the night when He was betrayed, the Lord Jesus took bread, gave thanks, broke it, and said, 'This is My body, which is for you. Do this in remembrance of Me'" (1 Cor 11:23–24). The language of receiving and passing on is technical language for a teaching orally given in the church for people to know and recall. The offer of the body on behalf of others is also explicit in Paul's version. The emphasis is on the fact that Jesus dies to open doors for others.

Listen to what Jesus said when He gave the cup to His disciples: "Then He took a cup, and after giving thanks, He gave it to them and said, 'Drink from it, all of you. For this is My blood that establishes the covenant; it is shed for many for the forgiveness of sins'" (Matt 26:27–28). Again, this is not suicide, but a sacrifice for the sake of others ("it is shed for many"), clearing the way for a covenant—which is to say, it points to a new relationship. Forgiveness leads to relationship. This is a core truth of the gospel that makes it good news. Jesus' death points to life and was designed that way from the beginning.

Luke speaks not just of the covenant but of the *new* covenant: "In the same way He also took the cup after supper and said, 'This cup is the new covenant established by My blood; it is shed for you'" (Luke 22:20). In the new covenant, discussed in the previous chapter, God forgives sins and writes His presence on our hearts. Paul's version in 1 Corinthians 11:25 is similar: "In the same way He also took the cup, after supper, and said, 'This cup is the new covenant in My blood. Do this, as often as you drink it, in remembrance of Me.'"

These scenes show how the Last Supper became the Lord's Supper. It commemorates at a community level the significance of Jesus' death. First Corinthians 10:16 says, "The cup of blessing that we bless, is it not a sharing in the blood of Christ? The bread that we break, is it not a sharing in the body of Christ?" Because of the way the Greek is worded, these questions expect a positive answer. We share with Jesus in His death. We are incorporated into Him and become a part of His new community. This is what Paul called the body of Christ, the people who now represent and share His presence in the world.

His death took our place and led to the forgiveness of our sins and the establishment of a promise God made long ago in the new covenant. Jesus' death was not merely about removing sin and its cost in guilt and death; it was about providing an unbroken fellowship with the living God. The meal shows that it is about far more than merely making a transaction to remove sin. In addition to providing the way for life, it also brings us into fellowship with God and His people. Here is a community meal that illustrates what the gospel's core is.

### The Lord's Table Is a Thanksgiving Meal

In the church of the generation after the apostles, this celebration became known as the Eucharist. That term refers to "thanksgiving," focusing on the relationship Jesus' work had established. One of the earliest of the post–New Testament works is called the *Didache*. Written in the late first or early second century, it summarizes the meal this way: "Now concerning the Eucharist, give thanks as follows. First, concerning the cup: We give you thanks, our Father, for the holy vine of David your servant, which you have made known to us through Jesus, your servant; to you be the glory forever. And concerning the broken bread: We give you thanks, our Father, for the life and knowledge which you have made known to us through Jesus, your servant; to you be the glory forever" (*Didache* 9:1–3). The meal was called explicitly a thanksgiving meal, a Eucharist. The prayer that comes with the elements shows that spirit of gratitude for experiencing the good news not merely as forgiveness but also in relationship with God. What has been gained is more important than what has been avoided.

Similar in force is the imagery of John 6 in the Bread of Life discourse, a text that pictures Jesus as the sustaining source and the One in whom we are called to believe. Just a portion of this discourse makes the point. In John 6:53–58 we see that the death of Jesus is about a new relationship:

"So Jesus said to them, 'I assure you: Unless you eat the flesh of the Son of Man and drink His blood, you do not have life in yourselves. Anyone who eats My flesh and drinks My blood has eternal life, and I will raise him up on the last day, because My flesh is real food and My blood is real drink. The one who eats My flesh and drinks My blood lives in Me, and I in him. Just as the living Father sent Me and I live because of the Father, so the one who feeds on Me will live because of Me. This is the bread that came down from heaven; it is not like the manna your fathers ate—and they died. The one who eats this bread will live forever.'" Manna had to be supplied daily. The Bread of Life is permanent, giving us life and sustaining it perpetually.

The table is to be a celebration of joy and gratitude for what God has done as we look forward to the rest of what He will do for His saved people. Paul says in 1 Corinthians 11:26, "For as often as you eat this bread and drink the cup, you *proclaim* the Lord's death until He comes."

The public celebration of this meal is actually both a personal and a corporate statement of God's alliance with us and our gratitude for being at the table in fellowship with Him. The corporate nature of the meal is stressed by Paul's warning to take this sacred meal in an appropriate manner by waiting to share in it together.

*Summary*
Many churches today probably do not celebrate the Lord's Table enough. This meal is the one commanded remembrance Jesus gave the church to reaffirm the community's roots and indebtedness to Him and His death. It brings to mind the depth of Jesus' sacrifice and the provision it supplied: forgiveness of sins *and* the establishment of the new covenant and era. The good news of the gospel points to relationship yet again in this meal. It portrays the acceptance of God and sees us as a community proclaiming together in symbolic act what God has done for us. When the church came to call this the Eucharist, they were highlighting the joy, celebration, and attitude the meal should generate. When I see the table presented in an almost quiet solemnity, I wonder if we have missed the point of its being a familial meal designed to declare where Jesus' death took us. Yes, the meal recalls a death, but it is a death that cleared a path into life. Yes, it was our sin that sent Him to die for us, innocent as He was, but Jesus did not die to remain on the cross. He died to be raised again into new life and become the triumphant Reconciler described in the hymn from Colossians 1:18–20:

> He is also the head of the body, the church;
> He is the beginning, the firstborn from the dead,
> so that He might come to have first place in everything.
> For God was pleased to have all His fullness dwell in Him,
> and through Him to reconcile everything to Himself
> by making peace through the blood of His cross—
> whether things on earth or things in heaven.

The first picture of the gospel focuses on Jesus' death not as an end, but as the beginning of a new era. It opens up the way to fellowship with God and entry into a new community with new possibilities to experience life as He designed it to be lived. That is good news indeed.

## Baptism: The Picture of Cleansing into New Life

Like the Lord's Supper, baptism illustrates what the gospel is all about. To appreciate it, we need to understand the role that washing, cleanliness, and purity played in Judaism.

*Purity and Washing in Judaism*

The picture of cleansing is tied to the promise of the new era even in the Old Testament. Through the prophet Ezekiel, God speaks of a sprinkling that cleanses and renews: "I will also sprinkle clean water on you, and you will be clean. I will cleanse you from all your impurities and all your idols. I will give you a new heart and put a new spirit within you; I will remove your heart of stone and give you a heart of flesh" (Ezek 36:25–26). This image of cleansing from impurity has a rich background in Jewish faith.

Uncleanness—related primarily to foods, childbirth, bodily discharges, and infection or disease—is treated in great detail in Leviticus 11–15. Some of the events associated with uncleanness were inevitable and so did not represent sin. Nevertheless, entry into uncleanness meant a person could not participate in worship of God at the tabernacle. The period of uncleanness varied depending on the circumstances. A person might be unclean until evening, as in the case of eating unclean food or touching anything associated with death. A mother who has given birth, on the other hand was unclean for forty to eighty days.

In the Levitical law, there are levels of uncleanness. Sometimes impurity was removed simply with the passing of time, but for other types of impurity, a washing or small sacrifice was required. Consider, for instance, the guidelines around the handling of a corpse, which are laid out in Numbers 19. A person who handles a corpse is unclean for seven days and has to have a ritual washing on the third and seventh days. When a person dies in a tent, anybody who is in the tent at the time of death is unclean for seven days. A person who handles the belongings of a dead person is unclean until evening. The priest who offers purifying water also has to wash his clothes.

All this uncleanness related to death is inevitable; people die, and somebody has to do something about the corpse. Nevertheless, that person is unclean, and his or her access to God is limited. The language is quite strong:

> Anyone who touches a body of a person who has died, and does not purify himself, defiles the tabernacle of the LORD. That person will be cut off from Israel. He remains unclean because the water for impurity has not been sprinkled on him, and his uncleanness is still on him. (Num 19:13)

Ultimately, this imagery of uncleanness is a portrayal of how special God is and how much honor He deserves. When a person is unclean, it takes time or a special washing to be able to reenter the presence of God. That is part of the point of the washing: to reenter a state where a person can approach God again.

Imagery like this stands behind Ezekiel's language about being sprinkled clean with water. The washing points to a clean state and being allowed to return to God's presence. Washing is not about hygiene or the removal of dirt. It is symbolism associated with a ritual state. Uncleanness reduces someone to a common level rather than being in a position of holiness. Being unclean and in need of washing meant a person was not in a ritual state and able to approach God's presence. All of this was designed to communicate the idea that approaching God was an honor.

*The Baptism of John the Baptist*
The baptism of John draws on the background of cleansing, but it also expands on it. The work of John was called a baptism of "repentance for the forgiveness of sins" (see also Luke 3:3). This was not a washing for the sake of a person's ritual status of everyday life; this was a washing that demonstrated the need and the desire for a moral cleansing associated with the arrival of the new era. It was the very kind of sprinkling Ezekiel promised. Although some have wanted to compare what John did with the kind of meticulous, ongoing, almost obsessively repetitive washing for cleanliness that took place among the Essenes—and especially at the separatist Jewish community of Qumran—there is no indication that John called for repeated washing.

Others have compared John's work to the washing that Gentiles would undergo when they wanted to become Jews. This was called *proselyte baptism*. However, we are not sure this was practiced as early as the first century. More important, John is appealing to other Jews who are in covenant with God and not entering Judaism for the first time. His appeal relates to the announcement we saw earlier: the One to Come follows John's ministry; washing is a way of preparing for God to come in this fresh new way. This washing could be called a *preparatory washing* for the new era. The call to repent was a call to embrace the holiness God's given Spirit would provide. John's baptism foreshadowed the inward cleansing by the Spirit. It also pointed to the fact that seeking forgiveness paved the way to experience a relationship with God. As we have seen before, forgiveness was never designed to stand alone; it took you to a new place with God.

### John 3: Water and the Spirit
Jesus also made this association. In John 3, he met with Nicodemus and spoke of being born anew from above, a birth associated with water. Jesus says to Nicodemus in verses 3–8,

> "I assure you: Unless someone is born again, he cannot see the kingdom of God."
>
> "But how can anyone be born when he is old?" Nicodemus asked Him. "Can he enter his mother's womb a second time and be born?"
>
> Jesus answered, "I assure you: Unless someone is born of water and the Spirit, he cannot enter the kingdom of God. Whatever is born of the flesh is flesh, and whatever is born of the Spirit is spirit. Do not be amazed that I told you that you must be born again. The wind blows where it pleases, and you hear its sound, but you don't know where it comes from or where it is going. So it is with everyone born of the Spirit."

Now, scholars debate what the water in this passage alludes to. Most see a connection to the cleansing imagery from Ezekiel, which is a reference not to baptism, but to a washing into spiritual cleanness that indicates new birth. Jesus' answer here stresses birth by the Spirit, not the role of the water. This emphasis is a reason interpreters prefer to emphasize the Spirit, but the mention of water does imply both a washing *and* the need for a fresh start in a relationship with God. Jesus is speaking with a rabbi who sought God every day, and yet even that rabbi had a need to enter into a new relationship with God that Jesus described as a new kind of life.

*Romans 6: Alive for God*
The same kind of imagery is also seen in Paul. In Romans 6:3–11, the apostle writes,

> Or are you unaware that all of us who were baptized into Christ Jesus were baptized into His death? Therefore we were buried with Him by baptism into death, in order that, just as Christ was raised from the dead by the glory of the Father, so we too may walk in a new way of life. . . . Now if we died with Christ, we believe that we will also live with Him, because we know that Christ, having been raised from the dead, no longer dies. Death no longer rules over Him. For in that He died, He died to sin once for all; but in that He lives, He lives to God. So, you too consider yourselves dead to sin, but alive to God in Christ Jesus.

There is much that could be said about this passage. A couple of themes are relevant to the gospel. First, those who embrace Jesus share in Jesus' death. The sin He bore—our sin—is buried with Him. Second, however, we are raised with Him into new life. Not only does Christ put sin to death in the sense that it can no longer make a claim on us, but He also overcomes death, inviting us to share life with Him. We are raised and can walk in a new way of life. This new life is what makes spiritual transformation possible. Baptism is the picture of that new, cleansed life in which we have reentered a relationship with God.

No wonder baptism became such a powerful image in the early church. When people believed, they often could not wait to be baptized to indicate the washing and new life in which they now participated. In the examples of the Ethiopian eunuch in Acts 8:36–38, Lydia and the Philippian jailer of Acts 16:15,33, or the family of Cornelius in Acts 10:48, people are baptized because they had affirmed in this one-time act the new life into which they had entered. That washing showed not only something left behind and put to death but also something else embraced and entered into. People who understood and appreciated the good news came to see themselves as "alive to God in Christ Jesus."

When people asked Peter what they should do in response to his initial gospel message, his reply was straightforward. "Repent," he said, "and be baptized, each of you, in the name of Jesus the Messiah for the forgiveness of your sins, and you will receive the gift of the Holy Spirit. For the promise is for you and for your children, and for all who are far off, as many as the Lord our God will call" (Acts 2:38–39).

Repent. Be baptized. Receive the Spirit.

*Another Explanation of the Picture of Baptism: First Peter 3*
Baptism does not save. What saves is God's action as it is pictured in baptism. Nothing says this more clearly than an explanation from the one who uttered the call to be baptized in Acts 2. In his first epistle, Peter turns his attention to baptism and explains how he sees it. As he discusses the gospel and even the need perhaps to suffer for embracing and proclaiming it, Peter invokes the example of Jesus and the picture of Noah being preserved in the flood. Here is how he says it in 1 Peter 3:14–22:

> But even if you should suffer for righteousness, you are blessed. Do not fear what they fear or be disturbed, but set apart the Messiah as Lord in your hearts, and always be ready to give a defense to anyone who asks you for a reason for the hope that is in you. However, do this with gentleness and respect, keeping your conscience clear, so that when you are accused, those who denounce your Christian life will be put to shame. For it is better to suffer for doing good, if that should be God's will, than for doing evil. (vv. 14-17)

First, note that we are all in the business of being ready to share the gospel's hope. We are all to be equipped to share the good news and to do so with a reflective self-understanding of what we share in. Second, the tone we do this with is as important as the message we speak. Peter exhorts us to share this hope with gentleness and respect, acting in a manner that leaves our conscience clear. We don't always see a tone of gentle respect in presentations of the gospel. Sometimes we are guilty of what I call Jimmy Cagney theology. Remember Cagney from the old black-and-white gangster movies? "You're the dirty rat that killed my brother." Sometimes when I hear people in the church share the gospel, the emphasis I hear is "You dirty rat! You shouldn't be doing that." We spend more time being sure people are convicted of sin than pointing them to the good news that overcomes it. This passage in Peter challenges that way of sharing the hope. The gospel is good news, and the stress should be on what makes it good news. The news is so good, in fact, that it's worth suffering for. As Peter says, "It is better to suffer for doing good, if that should be God's will, than for doing evil."

So what, exactly, is the gospel that is worth suffering for? Peter makes it clear:

> For Christ also suffered for sins once for all
> the righteous for the unrighteous,
> that He might bring you to God,
> after being put to death in the fleshly realm
> but made alive in the spiritual realm. (v. 18)

Jesus suffered and died, but suffering and death weren't an end in themselves. As we have already seen over and over, Christ's suffering and death brought new life and renewed relationship. In dying, Jesus' goal was to "bring people to God" and make people "alive in the spiritual realm." Even as Jesus suffered for sin, even as He showed how egregious sin was in the drama of salvation, the ultimate goal was not to convince people that they sinned but to point the way to God. Interestingly, what Peter says about the goal of Jesus' work matches what Paul said in Romans 6. The point is to make us alive and bring us to God.

And once again, the sign of this new life and new relationship is baptism. Baptism, according to Peter, "now saves you (not the removal of the filth of the flesh, but the pledge of a good conscience toward God) through the resurrection of Jesus Christ"

(1 Peter 3:21). It's not the water of baptism that does the work, Peter insists. Rather, that outward sign shows something that has happened on the inside—a cleansed conscience. That is the work of the Spirit inside a person. To be baptized is to come in faith to God to be washed clean from the inside out, knowing that this cleansing will bring you new life. And He has the authority to do it. The Jesus who came to us as a Man of sorrows, humble and meek, is now a mighty victor, as Peter proclaims: "Now that He has gone into heaven, He is at God's right hand, with angels, authorities, and powers subjected to Him" (v. 22).

*Summary*
Baptism is a picture of cleansing. The goal of this cleansing, as in the Old Testament, is to take us from a state of uncleanness to a state of cleanness before God. But in this new era, God goes one better than in the era of the law. Before, cleansing meant we were now capable of coming into God's presence in the tabernacle. In the new era, cleansing means that God gives us the new life of His Spirit and makes us into a new temple of His presence. In other words, we do not go to Him; He comes into us. In doing so, God makes us alive to Him.

## The Gospel Is about a Meal and a Cleansing

Two images regularly appear in the rites associated with church: one is a meal; the other is a washing. They also can be placed together. We are washed so that God can enter into our lives. He does so by the promise of His Spirit, the gift that indicates the new era. But this entry into our life also means we get to sit and sup at God's table. We are His children, members of His family. Our place at the table is made possible by Jesus' death. That opens the door to the fellowship hall of God. But death for sin is not the meal; it is the ticket to gain entry. Beyond that central transaction is the relationship. On the other side of Jesus' death, through which we have been cleansed, is the power and presence of fellowship with the living God. The Creator enters into our souls and makes us alive to Him. Whether we think of the picture of the Lord's Table or consider the washing depicted by baptism, we see an entry into communion with God and His people. To experience the cleansing and presence of the living God is good news.

## Questions for Discussion

1. How does the picture of the Lord's Table portray the gospel? What background comes from the Old Testament and how does Jesus alter it?
2. Is the Lord's Table more than a recollection of what Jesus did? Why do some call it the Eucharist?
3. How do washings and the issue of purity help us to understand the gospel?
4. What kind of washing was John's baptism?
5. What is key about Christian baptism in terms of the attitude of our heart in doing it? What does the coming up out of the water depict?
6. What difference does this theme make for me personally?

# Chapter 3

# A Unique Action Meeting
# a Comprehensive Need:
# The Cross

. . . . . . . . .

That Jesus died for our sin is probably the most highlighted feature of the church's preaching of the gospel. Yet sin has fallen on hard times in our world. The idea that we are accountable to a Creator, even if a person believes in a deity, is often seen to be passé. So in this chapter we examine why accountability to God is central to our interaction with Him. This accountability is what made the cross necessary: we are accountable to God, and yet by our nature we tend to go our own way and ignore God. That mismatch between our accountability and our actions is the starting point of all human need. The answer to that need begins with the cross.

## The Reason Behind the Cross: Tracing the Need

What does a relationship with God require? What does He expect? Four passages give us solid direction. One appears in Micah as God rebukes His people Israel for failing to be responsive to Him. A second sets the context for those remarks all the way back in the creation. The third shows Jesus' response to our unresponsiveness. The fourth tells us in no uncertain terms where all of us stand with God.

### Micah 6: God's Lawsuit
In Micah 6, God presents a lawsuit against His people, with all creation as witness. In indicating what God requires of His people,

God is explaining His call to them as His creatures. The text reflects God's desire and His displeasure.

"Now listen to what the LORD is saying:
  Rise, plead your case before the mountains,
  and let the hills hear your voice.
Listen to the LORD's lawsuit,
  you mountains and enduring foundations of the earth,
  because the LORD has a case against His people,
  and He will argue it against Israel.
My people, what have I done to you,
  or how have I wearied you?
Testify against Me! (vv. 1–3)

"What have I done wrong?" God asks of a people who have rejected Him, but they would have understood as well as we do that this is a rhetorical question. It is not God who has done wrong, but His people. No, God has been faithful to a people who have been unfaithful to Him. We are back again to the exodus:

Indeed, I brought you up from the land of Egypt
and redeemed you from that place of slavery.
I sent Moses, Aaron, and Miriam ahead of you.
My people,
remember what Balak king of Moab proposed,
what Balaam son of Beor answered him,
and what happened from Acacia Grove to Gilgal,
so that you may acknowledge
the LORD's righteous acts. (vv. 4–5)

"Remember," God says. That is what the Passover feast is about: remembering God's faithfulness, God's deliverance. As we have seen before, the remembrance of the Passover became the remembrance of the Lord's Supper ("Do this in remembrance of Me").

At this point, the perspective abruptly changes in the Micah passage. Now we hear not the voice of God speaking, but the voice of the sinner, as if God's call to remember has evoked a response:

What should I bring before the LORD
when I come to bow before God on high?
Should I come before Him with burnt offerings,
with year-old calves?
Would the LORD be pleased with thousands of rams,
or with ten thousand streams of oil?
Should I give my firstborn for my transgression,
the child of my body for my own sin? (vv. 6–7)

What can make restitution for people's failure to appreciate God's presence and goodness? Will it be rectified by sacrifices? Burnt offerings? The pouring out of oil? What about child sacrifice? Surely that would be a big enough sacrifice to please God. No, none of those is the answer. We human beings want the big gesture that we can do to make everything all right. But God doesn't want a big gesture. He wants something much simpler—and much harder. He wants us to walk, day by day, in accountability.

He has told you men what is good
and what it is the LORD requires of you:
Only to act justly,
to love faithfulness,
and to walk humbly with your God. (v. 8)

God asks us to show Him respect and to pass on that respect in the way we relate to others. Failing to do that is sin. God's problem with His people isn't their failure to sacrifice properly, but their willingness to take advantage of one another:

The voice of the LORD calls out to the city
(and it is wise to fear Your name):
"Pay attention to the rod
and the One who ordained it.
Are there still the treasures of wickedness
and the accursed short measure
in the house of the wicked?
Can I excuse wicked scales
or bags of deceptive weights?

> For the wealthy of the city are full of violence,
> and its residents speak lies;
> the tongues in their mouths are deceitful." (vv. 9–12)

Micah could have seen any of this same behavior by watching our daily news reports. We live in ways that do not reflect what God desires of those He created.

The rest of Micah 6 shows God does not ignore such behavior. He holds us accountable for it. Relationship with God is rooted in accountability to Him. God does not ignore the development of our character. If we go our own way, He sometimes allows us to reap the consequences of our choices, sometimes He intervenes to get our attention, but God always keeps us accountable even when we think we are completely free of His authority.

The judgment expressed in Micah 6:13–16 described God's response on this occasion:

> As a result, I have begun to strike you severely, bringing desolation because of your sins. You will eat but not be satisfied, for there will be hunger within you. What you acquire, you cannot save, and what you do save, I will give to the sword. You will sow but not reap; you will press olives but not anoint yourself with oil; and you will tread grapes but not drink the wine.

God judged at last. The nation saw that God does not ignore sin. Sometimes God judges immediately, sometimes that response waits until the end, but we are always accountable.

### Genesis 1: Made in His Image

Why does God care how we live? Why does He hold us accountable? He does so because of the way He made us. Genesis 1 pictures humanity as the pinnacle of the creation. Not the animals, not the earth, not even the heavens are made in the image of God. Only human beings hold that honor. Genesis 1:26–28 says it simply:

> Then God said, "Let Us make man in Our image, according to Our likeness. They will rule the fish of the sea, the birds of the

sky, the animals, all the earth, and the creatures that crawl on the earth." So God created man in His own image; He created him in the image of God; He created them male and female. God blessed them, and God said to them, "Be fruitful, multiply, fill the earth, and subdue it. Rule the fish of the sea, the birds of the sky, and every creature that crawls on the earth."

Humanity was created to reflect God and His rule. God gave to man and woman all creation to manage before Him. God gave us an environment to thrive in and the capability to make judgments to manage that world. Our role in "management" doesn't make us independent of God. Rather, it is all the more reason, as Micah said, "to walk humbly with your God."

Today, many people live as if God does not exist. They live to "do their own thing." The irony of that lifestyle is that "doing our own thing" is a denial of who we are at our core. We are beings who need to be in fellowship and relationship, and that includes a relationship with the One who created us. We were created to reflect Him. The rest of the early chapters of Genesis, the first eleven chapters in fact, show our consistent tendency to walk away from God and our relationship to Him. Whether we think of Adam, Cain, Noah, or the generation of the tower of Babel, we see humanity going the same way as the generation Micah addressed. There are murder, greed, selfishness, and all kinds of violence against others. It often is *our* way; we make selfish choices where God is left out of account. But God cared too much to leave it there.

It is here that God initiated the promise we noted earlier—His promise with Abraham to bless the earth. In that covenant, God promised to bless the earth with Abraham's seed. Through the nation Israel came the Promised One. It is His story the gospel tells. How does Jesus set up the gospel?

*Mark 12: The Great Commandment According to Jesus*
The foregoing discussion noted only a sampling of what could be presented on this theme of God's requirements and how we often respond to that demand. Jesus also addresses this idea. In Mark 12:28–34, Jesus and a scribe share a conversation about the most

important things. It is easy to get distracted in life and lose sight of its main purpose; a glance at this passage reminds us what is important to pursue throughout our lives. Here is the exchange:

> One of the scribes approached. When he heard them debating and saw that Jesus answered them well, he asked Him, "Which commandment is the most important of all?"
>
> "This is the most important," Jesus answered. "Listen, Israel! The Lord our God, The Lord is One. Love the Lord your God with all your heart, with all your soul, with all your mind, and with all your strength. The second is: Love your neighbor as yourself. There is no other commandment greater than these."
>
> Then the scribe said to Him, "You are right, Teacher! You have correctly said that He is One, and there is no one else except Him. And to love Him with all your heart, with all your understanding, and with all your strength, and to love your neighbor as yourself, is far more important than all the burnt offerings and sacrifices."
>
> When Jesus saw that he answered intelligently, He said to him, "You are not far from the kingdom of God."

This exchange takes us back to Micah 6. Loyalty to God and love for Him constitute the most important virtues in life. That loyalty expresses itself in loyalty to others as well. Jesus goes on to say that this loyalty puts us close to the kingdom of God. This loyalty drives us to pay attention to what God says, including what God says about love and sin. This loyalty causes a person to respond to the One whom God sent to deal with sin. It is no accident that this scene appears in Mark as Jesus is being challenged about who He is and who gave Him the right to do the things He claims to do. Jesus has come to represent God and bring the new era. He comes to meet that need for washing and cleansing that we discussed in the previous chapter. How deep does that need go? How far does it extend? One of God's greatest messengers, the apostle Paul, answers that question for us.

### Romans 3: A Second Lawsuit against Humanity

You may have been taught the "Roman Road" as a way of presenting the gospel, and for good reason. In the book of Romans, Paul offers one of the most clear and cogent presentations of the gospel in all of Scripture. Romans 1:18–3:18 declares our need. Romans 4–5 offers the answer to that need: we are declared righteous by faith, not works. Then in Romans 6–8, Paul discusses the gospel's ability to lead us into righteousness in practice.

Like Micah, Paul has a lawsuit of his own in Romans 3. He makes the case that every human being stands guilty before God if he or she has not responded to what God has done. In describing our guilt, Paul also describes our need in such a way that it is clear that only God can meet it through Jesus and the cross. This need is not to be avoided or denied, but to be embraced, for the depth of the need shows the beauty of the solution. Here is the lawsuit from Romans 3:9–18:

> What then? Are we any better? Not at all! For we have previously charged that both Jews and Gentiles are all under sin, as it is written:
>
> > There is no one righteous, not even one;
> > there is no one who understands,
> > there is no one who seeks God.
> > All have turned away,
> > together they have become useless;
> > there is no one who does good,
> > there is not even one.
> > Their throat is an open grave;
> > they deceive with their tongues.
> > Vipers' venom is under their lips.
> > Their mouth is full of cursing and bitterness.
> > Their feet are swift to shed blood;
> > ruin and wretchedness are in their paths,
> > and the path of peace they have not known.
> > There is no fear of God before their eyes.

This is a comprehensive indictment laid out in a very graphic way. Humanity, all of it, sins from head to toe. Whether we think of the tongue or the feet, all parts of us sin. Whether we think of Jew or Gentile, all of us sin. No one is innocent. We all have the same need. There is no fear of God, no loyalty. The main thing has become the forgotten thing, and we are accountable for our position. Now, that would be really grim news if there were no solution on the table. Thankfully, Paul goes on to explain this solution, as do other biblical writers. At the core of this solution is the cross.

John 3:16 says it directly: "For God loved the world in this way: He gave His One and Only Son, so that everyone who believes in Him will not perish but have eternal life." The indictment is not the end of the story, but the beginning. God did not leave the world to wallow in its faithlessness. The gospel is about God wooing the unfaithful back to Him. It is about love offered in the midst of scorn, designed to reverse a trend. We see the trend everywhere we look in our world: people turning their backs on who they were made to be and treating others—also precious and sacred reflections of the divine image—as objects. When Scripture says sin blinds and deceives, sin blinds us to the reality of our self-destructiveness. Sin tells us that we're really being ourselves, finding ourselves, when we really are acting selfishly.

Our need surrounds us and so overwhelms us that we call it "normal" and often become numb to it. We find it hard to look in the mirror and see our own faces. Yet at its core, loyalty to God requires that we confront what is right before our eyes. The great commandment tells us that only by being loyal to God will we also be able to get our relationship with His creatures right. As strange as it sounds, it is the suffering of one representative on a cross that reminds us of sin's cost, pays the price, and removes the guilt from the indictment God has brought against us all.

## The Solution: The Cleansing
## Offering of God's Own Beloved

Like John 3:16, Paul goes on in Romans to state briefly the solution to our dilemma of lost relationship to God. In Romans 3:21–24, he summarizes the core of the gospel in terms of the solution: "But now, apart from the law, God's righteousness has been revealed—attested by the Law and the Prophets—that is, God's righteousness through faith in Jesus Christ, to all who believe, since there is no distinction. For all have sinned and fall short of the glory of God. They are justified freely by His grace through the redemption that is in Christ Jesus."

Several terms in these verses are important. Some of the expressions, like "through faith in Jesus Christ" and "all who believe," are so important they will be explored in individual chapters. For now, let us focus on the transition from "all have sinned and fall short of the glory of God" to "the redemption that is in Christ Jesus." It is precisely here that the cross fits. It is the cross that secures the redemption, paying the penalty incurred by sin and clearing the way for a new relationship with God.

In some ways, we have already seen this idea. It was central to the symbolism of the Last Supper. Jesus inaugurated a new covenant in His blood. Old ways had gone; new rituals were provided. Let's look at what the New Testament has to say about the cross.

*First Corinthians 1: The Cross as God's Foolishness*
I imagine if you were to launch a public relations program on behalf of Jesus' work, the last place you would start would be to promote the cross as the foolishness of God! But that is exactly what Paul did. He did it because he understood that by any "normal" standards of evaluation, the cross seems strange. We briefly looked at this passage earlier but now consider it in detail to see the nature of Paul's appeal. First Corinthians 1:17–18 reads, "For Christ did not send me to baptize, but to preach the gospel—not with clever words, so that the cross of Christ will not be emptied of its effect. For to those who are perishing the message of the cross is foolishness, but to us who are being saved it is God's power."

The contrast between the way many perceive the cross and the way believers perceive it could not be clearer here. To the world, the cross seems foolish, even unnecessary. In the beginning of this chapter, I tried to explain why the cross is so very necessary; it pictures something essential about sin. Sin damages our relationship to God and requires an antidote. Yet to many—those who, according to Paul, prefer wisdom or signs—the cross makes no sense. Wisdom and signs have their own problems. Wisdom, at least the human kind, often operates independently from God, severing the core Creator–creature relationship that is the essence of human existence. Earthly wisdom says humanity can do whatever it wants in its own power through its own cleverness. In a sense, the cross is God's statement that such independence will never meet human need. The irony is that the very ability to reason is a key aspect of our being made in the image of God.

Through signs, on the other hand, we want to prove God, not to rely on Him. We want signs because we want a clear map. There is irony there as well. Despite what Paul says here, God gave signs all throughout Jesus' ministry. At several points in Jesus' career, people asked or looked for a sign (Matt 12:38; 16:1; Mark 8:11; Luke 11:29; John 2:18). But Jesus' whole life was a sign. When John the Baptist asked if Jesus was the One to Come, Jesus replied in Luke 7:22, "Go and report to John the things you have seen and heard: The blind receive their sight, the lame walk, those with skin diseases are healed, the deaf hear, the dead are raised, and the poor have the good news preached to them." These were nothing but indications of whom Jesus was—indications that the new era had come. In fact, John's Gospel is built on seven signs. But some wanted more, something of their own design. Paul said, in effect, "No—it's not for you to say what sign God should give you." The sign was the cross and everything that came with it—including a risen Jesus.

Another irony is that even Jewish tradition reports that Jesus had unusual power. In the material we have from the first century and beyond in Judaism, we are told about Jesus' power, which enabled Him to do unusual things. The late first-century Jewish historian Josephus tells us about a Jesus who was able to do "unusual" things (*Antiquities* 18.63–64). Justin Martyr in his debates with Jews notes how they attributed His unusual power not to God but to sorcery (Justin, *First Apology* 30, 108; *Contra Celsum* 1:28, 71; *Dialogue* 69:7). This skewed view of Jesus at least recognizes that Jesus did perform surprising acts. Later Jewish Talmudic tradition made similar claims (*b Sanh* 43a; 107b). And during His ministry, Jesus' enemies claimed that He cast out demons by the power of Beelzebul (Mark 3:22; Luke 11:15). No, Jesus answered, it makes no sense to believe that Satan casts out Satan; not even Satan would purposely fight against himself. Jesus' enemies were willing to do all sorts of mental gymnastics in order not to see the obvious meaning of Jesus' signs: His power came from God.

Paul refers to the cross as God's power because it is the means by which God gives new life and everything that goes with it. Paul says it best in 1 Corinthians 1:21–25:

> For since, in God's wisdom, the world did not know God through wisdom, God was pleased to save those who believe through the foolishness of the message preached. For the Jews ask for signs and the Greeks seek wisdom, but we preach Christ crucified, a stumbling block to the Jews and foolishness to the Gentiles. Yet to those who are called, both Jews and Greeks, Christ is God's power and God's wisdom, because God's foolishness is wiser than human wisdom, and God's weakness is stronger than human strength.

In verses 30–31, Paul explains how this works; he notes what accompanies the cross: "But from Him you are in Christ Jesus, who for us became wisdom from God, as well as righteousness, sanctification, and redemption, in order that, as it is written: The one who boasts must boast in the Lord." Here we see our key terms: *righteousness*, *sanctification*, and *redemption*. These come with the cross. When a person believes in the work Jesus performed on that piece of wood, God does three key things:

1. He declares that person righteous (i.e., He justifies him or her).
2. He sets that person apart as holy and one of His children. (He does this by giving them the Spirit that makes them saints, that is, He sets apart people for God.)
3. He redeems that person, having removed the debt and blot that sin is on one's soul.

This is why it is God's power and capability—not ours—that must stand behind our salvation. We do not earn it; He provides it as a gift. Nothing screams this louder than the cross, where Jesus paid for what I could not redeem on my own.

*Galatians 6, Ephesians 2, 1 Peter 1:*
*The Cross as a Rearrangement*
A few other passages in Paul indicate that an important goal of the cross is to "rearrange" our relationships. Galatians 6:14–15 speaks of being crucified to the world. In those verses, Paul says, "But may I never boast except in the cross of our Lord Jesus Christ, through which the world has been crucified to me, and I to the world. For neither circumcision nor uncircumcision counts for anything; the only thing that matters is a new creation!" (NET). In other words, the cross brought a realignment in our relationship to the world. We have died to what the world represents so that old battles—such as whether we are circumcised or not—do not impact how we view another. What counts is the new creation, that renewal of the relationship between God and those who respond to Jesus and His work—and consequently the renewal of the relationship between believers and those around them. This passage illustrates how the cross operates as a hub for Paul. It is not merely Jesus' death that is important but everything that radiates out of it. The spokes that extend out from the hub—those are the gospel too.

Ephesians 2 is in the same vein as Galatians 6. Here the issue is the reconciliation that grows out of Jesus' work on the cross. Jesus' death realigns the uneasy, even broken relationship between those who were near to the promise of God (the Jews) and those who were far away (the Gentiles):

> But now in Christ Jesus you who used to be far away have been brought near by the blood of Christ. For he is our peace, the one who made both groups into one and who destroyed the middle wall of partition, the hostility, when he nullified in his flesh the law of commandments in decrees. He did this to create in himself one new man out of two, thus making peace, and to reconcile them both in one body to God through the cross, by which the hostility has been killed. And he came and preached peace to you who were far off and peace to those who were near, so that through him we both have access in one Spirit to the Father. (vv. 13–18 NET)

Jesus brought a peace that did not previously exist between these two groups. In part, what had caused that separation was the law, which made them live so distinctly. Now Jesus is their peace.

Jesus' death reshuffled the cards for the Jews and Gentiles. Now both groups share the same Spirit, the same access to God. They are one new man, a picture of a unified person in Christ, showing how God made the two groups one. In Jesus' work on the cross, God has rearranged how people see and relate to each other.

Among the Church's earliest teachers, it wasn't just Paul who spoke of the cross reconfiguring our life. Listen to Peter in 1 Peter 1:17–19:

> And if you address as Father the One who judges impartially based on each one's work, you are to conduct yourselves in reverence during this time of temporary residence. For you know that you were redeemed from your empty way of life inherited from the fathers, not with perishable things, like silver or gold, but with the precious blood of Christ, like that of a lamb without defect or blemish.

Redemption reappears here, as does the reconfiguration brought by the death of Jesus. It changes everything about the way we conduct ourselves "during this time of temporary residence." What we are redeemed from is "an empty way of life." Paul was saying the same thing when he spoke of being "crucified to the world."

Why is this reconfiguration possible? Because Jesus was sacrificed like a spotless lamb—not temporarily, like the lambs of the old covenant, but once and for all. Peter emphasizes the fact that the work of Jesus stretches from the beginning of time to the end of time: "He was destined before the foundation of the world, but was revealed at the end of times for you who through Him are believers in God" (1 Pet 1:20–21). For Peter, as well as for the other writers of the New Testament, Jesus' work triggered the last days of God because His program took a turn from being promised to being realized. We saw this before when Peter quoted Joel in Acts 2 and noted these events take place in "these last days."

This collection of texts shows how Jesus' death, by God's design, rearranged things. Relationships with God, with other ethnic groups, and with the world are altered when we embrace what Jesus has done in His death. In short, the gospel is a game changer, placing us in a whole set of new relationships and calling us to reflect that change in the way we represent what God has done for us by His grace.

*Hebrews 8–10: Once and for All,*
*Inaugurating a New Covenant*
The book of Hebrews revolves around the idea that the work of Jesus on the cross gives better provision for sin than the law of the previous era. The anonymous author of Hebrews explains how Jesus is superior to the angels, better than Moses, more exalted than Aaron. The sacrifice of Jesus, he argues, was more comprehensive than all the millions of Old Testament sacrifices put together. Hebrews 8–10 is a key passage for understanding what Jesus' death meant. We'll begin with Hebrews 8:6–9:

> But now Jesus has obtained a superior ministry, since the covenant that he mediates is also better and is enacted on better promises. For if that first covenant had been faultless, no one would have looked for a second one. But showing its fault, God says to them, "Look, the days are coming, says the Lord, when I will complete a new covenant with the house of Israel and with the house of Judah. It will not be like the covenant that I made with their fathers, on the day when I took them by the hand to lead them out of Egypt, because they did not continue in my covenant and I had no regard for them, says the Lord. (vv. 6-9 NET)

As this passage makes clear, a new era is overtaking the former one. The new covenant mediates better promises. And those better promises include a change from the inside out—a change that results in a whole new intimacy between God and His people. Through Christ, we have access to God that we never had before:

"For this is the covenant that I will establish with the house of
Israel after those days, says the Lord. I will put my Laws in their
minds and I will inscribe them on their hearts. And I will be
their God and they will be my people. And there will be no need
at all for each one to teach his countryman or each one to teach
his brother saying, 'Know the Lord,' since they will all know me,
from the least to the greatest. For I will be merciful toward their
evil deeds, and their sins I will remember no longer." (vv. 10-12
NET)

These are amazing promises. The once-and-for-all sacrifice of
Jesus gives us an ongoing intimacy with the God of the universe.
God dwells inside us.

In 10:19–22 (NET), the author of Hebrews puts together much
of what we have already said about the gospel:

Therefore, brothers and sisters, since we have confidence to
enter the sanctuary by the blood of Jesus, by the fresh and living
way that he inaugurated for us through the curtain, that is,
through his flesh, and since we have a great priest over the house
of God, let us draw near with a sincere heart in the assurance
that faith brings, because we have had our hearts sprinkled clean
from an evil conscience and our bodies washed in pure water.

Jesus' death opens up a new path into God's throne room. The
sanctuary is heaven, where God dwells and Jesus sits like a high
priest over that house, mediating the blessings we receive by
God's kindness. This work gives us permission to draw near; it
gives us *access*, as Paul puts it in Ephesians 2. We can draw near
because our hearts are sprinkled and our bodies are washed,
images we discussed in the previous chapter.

Earlier, in verses 10–11, the author of Hebrews makes another
important point about what Jesus' death achieved. The law, he
says, gives but a shadow of the things to come. The repeated
sacrifices of the Old Testament pointed to the once-and-for-all
sacrifice of Jesus: "By this will, we have been sanctified through
the offering of the body of Jesus Christ once and for all. Now
every priest stands day after day ministering and offering time
after time the same sacrifices, which can never take away sins."

The author drives home the uniqueness and completeness of Jesus' sacrifice in verses 12–14 (NET): "But when this priest had offered one sacrifice for sins for all time, he sat down at the right hand of God, where he is now waiting until his enemies are made a footstool for his feet. For by one offering he has perfected for all time those who are made holy." Jesus' death accomplished something permanent. The reconfiguration that comes in the gospel needs no supplements. All that is needed to accomplish salvation is provided in what He did once and for all.

## Summary: Meeting a Comprehensive Need with a Unique Act

So the cross is precious to the church and has been for all time. It represents a consummate act of love performed to rescue humanity from a deep, crying need. This need does not call for finger wagging or mean-spirited address. It represents a deep flaw and tragic failing in all of us. It is a need and a debt we cannot fix on our own. All this would be tragic if we were doomed to be stuck in it. But we are not.

Jesus' death showed how committed God was to recovering the lost and restoring the image of God into its original design. His death redeemed us and took care of the debt and guilt. Jesus made this transaction on our behalf as our representative in death. But that was not all Jesus did. He also restored us into a new way, bringing new relationship, new power, and new access to the living God. In addition, He reconfigured our relationship so we could play a constructive role in our world and for each other.

In delivering us for God and to Him, Jesus also delivered us back to each other. The church that understands the depth of Jesus' death can never cease to speak of what He did on the cross, as well as what grows out of that unique death. The reversal is too great; the reconfiguration is too awesome. In one unique act, Jesus dealt with our universal need once and for all. In one act, tragedy became victory. This too is why the gospel, even as it relates to sin, ultimately is good news. It is because in Jesus, sin does not have the last word, redemption does. For in Jesus' unique work, He forged a pathway out of the grasp of sin and death into God's home and place of peace. The depth of the debt only serves to accentuate the height of the glory. Jesus' meeting a comprehensive need with this unique act of reversal is good news.

## Questions for Discussion

1. What does God ask of people according to Micah, and how does that tie into the gospel?
2. How does the gospel relate to Genesis 1?
3. What does the great commandment have to do with the gospel?
4. What lawsuit does God bring against humanity?
5. The cross provides forgiveness, but what relational dimension does it bring that fuels the gospel?
6. What impact does the cross bring to relationships?
7. What relationship does the cross have to the covenants?
8. What difference does this theme make for me personally?

# Chapter 4

# The Gospel Is Inaugurated as a Gift of God's Grace

* * * * * * * * *

The best-known hymn in the United States is surely "Amazing Grace." This hymn is sung on all kinds of occasions. It has become a part of cultural Christianity. However, it is a solid choice. As well as any piece of Christian hymnody, this hymn summarizes what the gospel reflects: the amazing grace of God. Salvation is a gift of God's underserved kindness toward us. In this chapter, we will examine this central gospel theme. In this hymn, the composer makes it clear that we did not earn our salvation. Rather, God rescued us: "Amazing grace, how sweet the sound that saved a wretch like me. I once was lost, but now am found, was blind but now I see."

Paul says the same thing in Romans 5:6-8: "For while we were still helpless, at the appointed moment, Christ died for the ungodly. For rarely will someone die for a just person—though for a good person perhaps someone might even dare to die. But God proves His own love for us in that while we were still sinners Christ died for us!" These verses connect with what we covered in the last chapter, Jesus' death for sin. Our new life came when we were helpless. Jesus' offer was extended to us when we were not responding to God as we should, but He never turned His back on us; instead, He gave His life for ours. That is grace, undeserved favor, merit given where it was not deserved. The gratitude this grace engenders is also seen in the words of the hymn. This is not merely grace; it is amazing and sweet. That is the love of God expressed in the gospel.

### Relationship with God by the Gift of His Grace

*Acts 2: The Gift of Relationship*
When we discussed Acts 2 earlier, I noted we would have to look at it more than once. Earlier we cited it as a text about the promise of renewed relationship with God. Now, we look at it again to examine what it says about the gospel being a gift.

In his sermon, Peter had noted that God promised through Joel that His Spirit would come to indwell His people. He then went on to note how Jesus' resurrection had been pictured in Psalm 16. Death could not hold Jesus. And why was He raised? He was raised to be exalted, to be at God's right hand and bestow the gift of this promised relationship on those who came to God to receive it. Peter develops this argument in Acts 2:22–36:

> "Men of Israel, listen to these words: Jesus the Nazarene, a man clearly attested to you by God with powerful deeds, wonders, and miraculous signs that God performed among you through him, just as you yourselves know—this man, who was handed over by the predetermined plan and foreknowledge of God, you executed by nailing him to a cross at the hands of Gentiles.
>
> "But God raised him up, having released him from the pains of death, because it was not possible for him to be held in its power. For David says about him:
>
>> 'I saw the Lord always in front of me,
>> for he is at my right hand so that I will not be shaken.
>> Therefore my heart was glad and my tongue rejoiced;
>> my body also will live in hope,
>> because you will not leave my soul in *Hades*,
>> nor permit your Holy One to *experience decay*.
>> You have made known to me the paths of life;
>> you will make me full of joy with your presence.'
>
> "Brothers, I can speak confidently to you about our forefather David, that he both died and was buried, and his tomb is with us to this day.

"So then, because he was a prophet and knew that God had sworn to him with an oath to seat one of his descendants on his throne, David by foreseeing this spoke about the resurrection of the Christ, that he was neither abandoned to *Hades*, nor did his body *experience decay*. This Jesus God raised up, and we are all witnesses of it.

"So then, exalted to the *right hand* of God, and having received the promise of the Holy Spirit from the Father, he has poured out what you both see and hear. For David did not ascend into heaven, but he himself says,

"'The Lord said to my *lord*,

""'Sit at my *right hand*, until I make your enemies a footstool for your feet.'"

"Therefore let all the house of Israel know beyond a doubt that God has made this Jesus whom you crucified both *Lord* and Christ!" (NET; emphasis added to show verbal links)

This passage ties together texts from the Hebrew Scripture, namely, Psalms 16 and 110, with the events of Jesus' life. I have shown these links in the italics of the previous citation. It says in effect that Jesus' life was living out a program God had previously revealed. It says that the crucifixion wasn't something that just happened *to* Jesus. It was the plan all along.

This outpouring was a gift. Acts 2:38 says it directly in calling for a response to what God had done: "Peter said to them, 'Repent, and each one of you be baptized in the name of Jesus Christ for the forgiveness of your sins, and you will receive the gift of the Holy Spirit'" (NET). The gift was the direct result of Jesus being taken to God's side after the resurrection so that He could distribute that promised gift to those who humbly came to receive it. This is the narrative core of the gospel. Jesus went from death for sin to life. That life went to the right hand of God. Receiving the Spirit from God's right hand, Jesus poured it out as a gift. The promise of God comes to those who come to Him to receive what He freely gives. At the center of the gift is the Spirit, from the Father through the Son. It is grace, pure and simple. It is amazing because we do not earn it; God graciously gives life in the Spirit through Jesus.

If there is a hard thing to grasp and appreciate about the gospel, it is the idea that we do not earn it. We are used to earning what we get (or taking it for ourselves), so we expect honor before God to be something we earn. Gifts do not come easily in our world. We take pride in securing what we get the old-fashioned way—by earning it. However, this is not the gospel. The gospel is that God gave us what we did not deserve, making it all the more precious. It was not what was owed us; it was what God desired for us to receive. Other passages also reinforce this point.

### Romans 4: Given, Not Earned

Another key text explaining the gospel as a gift comes in the continuing narrative Paul gives to the gospel in Romans 4. Here Abraham and David are presented as examples of the gift of grace and the role of faith in salvation. Abraham is discussed first in Romans 4:1–5:

> What then can we say that Abraham, our forefather according to the flesh, has found?
> If Abraham was justified by works, then he has something to brag about—but not before God. For what does the Scripture say?
> Abraham believed God,
> and it was credited to him for righteousness.
> Now to the one who works, pay is not considered as a gift, but as something owed.
> But to the one who does not work, but believes on Him who declares righteous the ungodly, his faith is credited for righteousness.

Abraham was not declared righteous (justified) by works of the law; rather God credited righteousness to his account in response to Abraham's believing God. The Scripture Paul cites is Genesis 15:6. As Paul points out, when we are given something as a reward for work done, that is not a gift. The salvation that comes to us by faith is a gift from God, not a reward. We are judged righteous when we believe the One who alone can make us righteous—the One who is eager to give us that gift.

Paul's picture of David is similar. Consider Romans 4:6–8:

Likewise, David also speaks of the blessing of the man to whom God credits righteousness apart from works:

> How happy those whose lawless acts are forgiven
> and whose sins are covered!
> How happy the man whom
> the Lord will never charge with sin!

Again, the emphasis is that works do not earn salvation, but are a gift: faith is credited as righteousness. The passage Paul quotes is from Psalm 32:1–2. Notice the passive verbs: *are forgiven, are covered*. It is God who is at work, not us. As Paul says elsewhere, the idea that it is not our labors that save us and bring us happiness is foolishness in the world's eyes. But that is the gospel.

Paul then comes back to discuss Abraham in detail. The point he makes is that Abraham was credited with being righteous before he was circumcised. In other words, God blessed Abraham with righteousness before he was obedient to the law and performed circumcision. Romans 4:9–10 says it this way: "Is this blessing only for the circumcised, then? Or is it also for the uncircumcised? For we say, faith was credited to Abraham for righteousness. How then was it credited—while he was circumcised, or uncircumcised? Not while he was circumcised, but uncircumcised." It truly is remarkable what God did in the life of Abraham before Abraham ever performed one act of obedience. From Genesis to Revelation, Scripture shows that salvation is a gift and comes through faith, not works from the law.

*Galatians 1–2: Paul Rebukes Some*
*Who Seek Salvation by Works of the Law*
Perhaps the angriest letter in the New Testament is Galatians. Paul is furious with a church he helped plant because some are seeking to convince the body that they need to keep the law to be saved. So strong is his reaction to this alternative way of explaining the gospel that he declares in Galatians 1:6–8, "I am amazed that you are so quickly turning away from Him who called you by the grace of Christ, and are turning to a different gospel—not that there is another gospel, but there are some who are troubling you and want

to change the gospel of Christ. But even if we or an angel from heaven should preach to you a gospel other than what we have preached to you, a curse be on him!'"

Those are strong words: a curse on anyone who preaches a different gospel? Even if that person is an angel? Any presentation of the gospel that adds human works to God's grace is not the gospel—and is worthy of bringing a curse down on the speaker. Any gospel based on works is an anti-gospel.

In Galatians 2, he develops the point. Verse 16 says, "Yet we know that no one is justified by the works of the law but by faith in Jesus Christ. And we have believed in Christ Jesus, so that we might be justified by faith in Christ and not by the works of the law, because by the works of the law no human being will be justified." Once again, it is said without any ambiguity. Being declared righteous by God is the product not of what we do with law but of faith in Jesus Christ. Works justify no one.

A few verses later, Paul drives the point home even more. In verse 21, he says, "I do not set aside the grace of God; for if righteousness comes through the law, then Christ died for nothing." If salvation is by works of the law, then Jesus had no reason to die. There was no need for Him to cover our sins; we could cover it ourselves. In other words, to seek to be justified by our own labor is to tell God He did not need to send His Son to die in our place. All that work and sacrifice was not needed.

However, God *did* undertake this labor of love. The fact that He did it at all is evidence that it was utterly necessary. Who would jump in the water to save a drowning man if he knew the drowning man could save himself? Salvation has to come at God's initiative because we cannot fix our sin problem without His gracious work on our behalf. Even the giving of God's law could not fix the problem. In fact in Galatians 5:4, Paul says that those "trying to be justified by the law are alienated from Christ" and "have fallen from grace." It is not grace *and* works or grace *and* anything that makes us righteous. It is—it can be—only grace.

*Ephesians 2: A Review of Salvation as a Work of Grace*
Ephesians 2:1–10 has perhaps the most famous passage presenting the gospel as a product of God's grace. Here the entire work of Christ is reviewed from where it starts to where it takes us. Our condition at the beginning is a key to the entire picture. We start out dead because of sin, so only God can bring us back to life:

> And you were dead in your trespasses and sins in which you previously walked according to this worldly age, according to the ruler of the atmospheric domain, the spirit now working in the disobedient. We too all previously lived among them in our fleshly desires, carrying out the inclinations of our flesh and thoughts, and by nature we were children under wrath, as the others were also.
>
> But God, who is abundant in mercy, because of His great love that He had for us, made us alive with the Messiah even though we were dead in trespasses. By grace you are saved! He also raised us up with Him and seated us with Him in the heavens, in Christ Jesus, so that in the coming ages He might display the immeasurable riches of His grace in His kindness to us in Christ Jesus. For by grace you are saved through faith, and this is not from yourselves; it is God's gift—not from works, so that no one can boast. For we are His creation—created in Christ Jesus for good works, which God prepared ahead of time so that we should walk in them.

It could hardly be clearer. We were spiritually dead before God. We were absolutely powerless to do anything on our own behalf. The "you" and "we" in this passage are Gentiles and Jews, respectively. All had sinned, Paul told us in Romans 3, and the apostle tells us the same thing here in different words. In the midst of this terrible dilemma, God shows up. He shows up full of mercy. Mercy is something God does because He wants to, not because He has to. He shows up full of love. God chooses to make us alive in Christ. God gives us a place with Him in heaven, making us a part of His family. So in the end, salvation is His gift, not from works. Those who benefit from God's grace are the work of His creative hands, experiencing a new life in a new birth, what Scripture calls elsewhere "being born from above" or "born again."

And yet, despite all Paul says about works, he does not throw them away. This is another part of Paul's teaching we often miss.

Works are a product of the new life of faith. Faith saves and faith works. We were "created in Christ Jesus for good works, which God prepared ahead of time so that we should walk in them." Why does God save us? So that we can again be useful, fulfilling the design that He originally had for us. That is true fulfillment—walking in the purpose for which we were made. Good works are the indicator that salvation has taken place. When we are born again, we are God's creation, His living poems. The word for *creation* in Ephesians 2:10 describes something someone else, in this case God, has brought into existence. We are designed for good works. We are built to serve and be useful. God designed this path so that having been saved and enabled in this new relationship, we can now walk in the good labor He designed for us originally to perform.

This passage is extremely significant. It not only summarizes and clarifies the truth that salvation is God's gift of grace through faith, but it also points us to a life of positive labor for God. It is perfectly balanced: It says yes to faith, yes to grace, and yes to works that grow out of a renewed heart realigned to the living God.

### Titus 2 and 3: Summaries of God's Grace

Titus 2 might be the crispest summary of God's grace in all the New Testament. In it, Paul tells us all that grace seeks to achieve:

> For the grace of God has appeared, with salvation for all people, instructing us to deny godlessness and worldly lusts and to live in a sensible, righteous, and godly way in the present age, while we wait for the blessed hope and the appearing of the glory of our great God and Savior, Jesus Christ. He gave Himself for us to redeem us from all lawlessness and to cleanse for Himself a special people, eager to do good works. (vv. 11–14)

The offer of grace instructs as it calls. Grace calls us to a sensible, godly life until Jesus returns to finish the salvation and redemption of the world His work started. His death had two goals: (1) to redeem us from lawlessness—that is, to lead us into wise living—and (2) to produce a washing that created a special people, a topic we treated in more detail in an earlier chapter. This special people has a heart that is eager to do good works. Again, we see how grace as a gift was designed to inspire people to live well and do good.

Sometimes works are seen negatively in the church. They are seen as obscuring grace. This concern is true only when works replace grace or faith. However, when works show the presence of God's grace activated in faith they reflect the very intent God had in making salvation a gift.

A second passage in Titus is also instructive. Here the focus is on the Spirit that is so crucial and central to what the gospel supplies. Titus 3:4–7 indicates what is gained when the gospel is received as a gift:

> But when the goodness and love for man appeared from God our Savior, He saved us—not by works of righteousness that we had done, but according to His mercy, through the washing of regeneration and renewal by the Holy Spirit. This Spirit He poured out on us abundantly through Jesus Christ our Savior, so that having been justified by His grace, we may become heirs with the hope of eternal life.

Again, the key image is one of cleansing. This washing led to regeneration or what Scripture also calls "being born again." The renewal into life takes place through the Spirit that was poured out through Jesus. Remember what Peter said at Pentecost in Acts 2. Jesus, at the right hand of God, poured out this Spirit on God's people. The result is that we are declared righteous by God's grace and we receive a place in the family of God as heirs who one day will experience eternal life. The themes of Spirit, washing, grace, and relationship to God are heard again and again in these passages on the gospel.

### First Peter 1: A Divine Program

So far, the bulk of our texts about the gospel as grace come from Paul, but he is not alone in seeing grace at work in the gospel. We have heard the preaching of Peter in Acts 2, but in his letters, he also writes about God's grace. First Peter opens with a note of praise for what God has done for His people: "Blessed be the God and Father of our Lord Jesus Christ. According to His great mercy, He has given us a new birth into a living hope through the resurrection of Jesus Christ from the dead, and into an inheritance that is imperishable, uncorrupted, and unfading, kept in heaven for you, who are being protected by God's power through faith for a salvation that is ready to be revealed in the last time" (1 Pet 1:3–5). Themes Paul rang are affirmed in Peter. There is the new birth, the regeneration by God's Spirit. There is the note of hope that is tied to sharing in an inheritance as a member of God's family. There is the role of faith in it all. All of this is done by God's mercy. Another way to say this is God's gift and kindness stand behind the gospel.

This praise is associated with the gospel a few verses later when Peter affirms that what has been declared matches up with what the prophets had promised. First Peter 1:10–12 notes that the prophets of old were foreshadowing what God would do through the Christ:

> Concerning this salvation, the prophets who prophesied about the grace that would come to you searched and carefully investigated. They inquired into what time or what circumstances the Spirit of Christ within them was indicating when He testified in advance to the messianic sufferings and the glories that would follow. It was revealed to them that they were not serving themselves but you concerning things that have now been announced to you through those who preached the gospel to you by the Holy Spirit sent from heaven. Angels desire to look into these things.

The gospel is precious. It is rooted in the two-part career of the Christ, the One who suffered first and was exalted afterward. These prophets did not put the entire puzzle of God's program together, but they did give us pieces in their writings. Now that Jesus had brought it all together, the good news of the gospel of God's grace could be proclaimed.

*Jude: A Warning about Abusing Grace*

Jude is probably one of the least well-known of the New Testament books. It is a single chapter and is full of warnings about those who lead the church astray. The threat discussed is teaching that leads to immorality. Jude invokes the past examples of Sodom and Gomorrah as he warns of those who will try to take the gospel and make it into something that becomes an excuse to do what we please rather than something that leads into righteousness. This is an approach God rejects; He will meet it with judgment.

Jude warns believers they cannot abuse grace without paying a price. Jude 3–4 issues this warning: "Dear friends, although I was eager to write you about our common salvation, I found it necessary to write and exhort you to contend for the faith that was delivered to the saints once for all. For certain men, who were designated for this judgment long ago, have come in by stealth; they are ungodly, turning the grace of our God into promiscuity and denying our only Master and Lord, Jesus Christ." Grace is precious. It cannot be treated as something common, something to note in passing as we go on living as though nothing matters but what we want or desire. When we treat grace as only a transaction and forget its design for the renewed life the Spirit gives, we deny the very rationale for embracing that grace, which can indicate perhaps that we never embraced it in the first place. We show that what we wanted was not the new life, but a ticket for the liberty to live how we pleased. To do that is not to embrace the gospel but to reject the very Master and Lord who provided it.

We need only review why Jesus died and why the gift was given to understand that grace is not a free ticket to do what we want. Jude warns the church about those who teach in this manner. At the end of his letter in verses 17–19, Jude says this about such teachers: "But you, dear friends, remember the words foretold by the apostles of our Lord Jesus Christ; they told you, 'In the end time there will be scoffers walking according to their own ungodly desires.' These people create divisions and are merely natural, not having the Spirit." Jude could not be clearer: the Spirit, so central a benefit of the gospel, does not reside in people who teach such an abuse of grace. So Jude calls his readers to live faithfully by building themselves in the faith, praying in the Spirit, and keeping themselves in love with God. They are to have mercy on those who doubt, snatch others from fire, and have compassion with fear on those who are unrighteous. In other words, grace is something to honor with a life worthy of God and His grace.

## Jesus as Word: The Unique Bearer of Grace

*John 1: Another Summary of Grace*
We live in a world where diversity is a cherished value. One of the characteristics of such a world is that all religions and religious claims are leveled out—treated as if they were just so many equally legitimate paths to get to the same place. But we must not miss the uniqueness of God's work of grace through Jesus. I am writing this chapter in Jordan, where I am teaching for a few weeks at an evangelical seminary that serves the Arab world. In this part of the world, like so many other places, Jesus is treated with respect, but Islam shows respect by treating Jesus as one among many prophets of God. But that is not what Christianity claims. To truly respect Jesus is to take Him at His word. At least, this is what John's Gospel teaches.

The grace of God centers in the activity of a unique figure, a one-of-a-kind being, what John's Gospel calls "the Word became flesh." In addition, the revelation of God's grace comes in and through this unique One, "the only begotten" or "One and Only" of the Father. There had never been anyone like Jesus before, nor has there been anyone like Him since. This Jesus is the custodian of God's grace. We close this chapter on grace by considering who He is. This will also be the subject of the next chapter as we show how the earliest believers made the case for Jesus' uniqueness.

John's Gospel says it directly in 1:1–18. Jesus is the Word, the One who is and reveals God. I am laying out the passage with its structure in distinct lines so we can see the argument laid out a point at a time:

> In the beginning was the Word,
> and the Word was with God,
> and the Word was God.

He was with God in the beginning.
All things were created through Him,
and apart from Him not one thing was created
that has been created.
Life was in Him,
and that life was the light of men.
That light shines in the darkness,
yet the darkness did not overcome it.
There was a man named John
who was sent from God.
He came as a witness
to testify about the light,
so that all might believe through him.
He was not the light,
but he came to testify about the light.
The true light, who gives light to everyone,
was coming into the world.
He was in the world,
and the world was created through Him,
yet the world did not recognize Him.
He came to His own,
and His own people did not receive Him.
But to all who did receive Him,
He gave them the right to be children of God,
to those who believe in His name,
who were born,
not of blood,
or of the will of the flesh,
or of the will of man,
but of God.
The Word became flesh
and took up residence among us.
We observed His glory,
the glory as the One and Only Son from the Father,
full of grace and truth.
(John testified concerning Him and exclaimed,
"This was the One of whom I said,
'The One coming after me has surpassed me,
because He existed before me.'")
Indeed, we have all received grace after grace

from His fullness,
for although the law was given through Moses;
grace and truth came through Jesus Christ.
No one has ever seen God.
The One and Only Son—
the One who is at the Father's side—
He has revealed Him.

John does not wait to say that Jesus was God. He says it in the very first verse. What God was, Jesus was. He was before the creation and participated in the creation, making Him every bit the Creator the Father is, even one who could be associated with life itself. That life that He could generate was like a light in darkness. That light, testified to by the witness John the Baptist, came into the world from outside of it. This is no creature we are discussing. He came into the world not as a part of it, but as a Creator of it.

He came to His own people, the Jews, but the bulk of them were not receptive to Him. That did not matter. Those who received His message were called God's children. They are those who believe in the power of His name, that is, of His person. These are those born into new life by the will of God. This is yet another way to say that salvation is by the grace of God; it is His activity that generates the new life. This Word took on the limitations of human existence and dwelt among the people He had created. How the infinite can inhabit the finite is one of the great mysteries of the faith. But the One who creates life can certainly choose to function in it as He wishes.

This Word, Jesus, was full of grace and truth, a visible manifestation of the glory and presence of God. This is One who existed before John the Baptist even though His birth came after John was born. From this unique One we receive nothing but grace after grace as God pours out His gifts of favor on those who are His. God's law had come with Moses, but it is in Jesus that we best see encapsulated the grace and truth that comes from God. No one sees God in a direct way but the One and Only Son, the unique One who is at God's side and has disclosed God to the world. That is precisely why Jesus can be called "the Word."

Everything about grace rotates around Jesus. He brings it. He shows it. He gives it. The Christian message at its core is not about a religious institution, about humanity earning its way into God's presence. Nor is the gospel a feel-good faith created to meet human desires independent of God. Christianity is far too honest about human need and frailty to be defined by such human desires. The Christian gospel is the story of a loving and gracious God taking the initiative to fix what we cannot fix ourselves. It is an act of His pure mercy, love, and grace. Undeserved but openly offered, God's grace serves as an invitation to enter into the courts of heaven as a family member of God with washings and provisions only God can give. With forgiveness behind us, the Spirit in us, and life everlasting in front of us, the gospel is good news offered in the hope it will be received. By embracing faith, the person receiving grace says, "I want what only God can give—new life. I want what only God could supply—undeserved but graciously given fellowship with the One who created all of us." The care of the Creator reflects grace that is truly amazing. It is good news that deserves a response.

## Questions for Discussion

1. Why is the gospel called a gift, and what promise is it tied to in Acts 2?
2. Why do works of the law obscure appreciating the origin of the gospel?
3. Paraphrase what it means to be "born again" according to Ephesians 2.
4. Why are works (not works of the law) related to the gospel and how?
5. What does the gospel teach us to do and to be?
6. What does Jude warn about abusing the gospel?
7. What does John 1 tell us about grace?
8. What difference does this theme make for me personally?

# Chapter 5

# The Gospel Is Affirmed in Divine Action and Scripture: God Showing Who Jesus Is

• • • • • • • • •

In 1 Corinthians 15:3–5, Paul declares that the death and resurrection stand at the crossroads of the gospel story. These events are part of the new community's earliest traditions. Paul declares, "For I passed on to you as of first importance what I also received—that Christ died for our sins according to the scriptures, and that he was buried, and that he was raised on the third day according to the scriptures, and that he appeared to Cephas, then to the twelve" (NET). Two events are said to really indicate who Jesus is: His death for sin and His being raised by God. The relationship of these two events and how Jesus set them up as key are the focus of this chapter.

By telling that story I also hope to show how and why the church argued that Jesus truly was unique, a one-of-a-kind figure unlike any other religious luminary the world has ever seen. In this story comes the explanation of why the church came to confess and see Jesus as God. Bear in mind, this faith emerged from Judaism, which confessed as a basic tenet that there is only one God. Every Sabbath, Jews recite the Shema from Deuteronomy 6:4: "Listen, Israel: The LORD our God, the LORD is one." The claim that a man could be God stretched the limits of Judaism. How could anyone hold to both Judaism and Christianity as the earliest Jewish believers in Jesus did?

This chapter will differ from the previous chapters of this book. Our study up to this point has concentrated on key individual

passages that expound our theme. In this chapter, we will highlight some specific events that reveal who Jesus is. This chapter
proceeds in four parts. First, we will look at an incident in Jesus'
life that is key to pursuing this question. Second we will consider
how these events helped the earliest believing community see this
relationship between God and Jesus. Third, we will analyze a text
that likely was a hymn sung in the early church, which also
addresses this issue. Finally, we look at how a key creed in Judaism
is restructured to make clear Jesus' importance and position. The
central question is this: Is it "kosher" to substitute Jesus into God's
place? If so, what does that mean for the gospel? In addition, how
do we present and talk about Jesus to those for whom this move
seems so radical (and even inappropriate)?

## Mark 14: The Confrontation with the
## Jewish Leadership That Led to the Cross

We will first consider Jesus' examination by the Jewish leadership, an
interview that ended up with the leaders deciding to take Jesus to
Pilate. These leaders asked Rome to crucify Jesus. In a sense, this is
the scene that tells us why Jesus was crucified. Much has brought
Jesus to this place. He has had numerous encounters with the leadership over issues related to Jewish practice. He has claimed to forgive
sin, something only God can do (Mark 2:1–12). He has acted on the
Sabbath in ways the scribes and Pharisees saw as violations of Sabbath
rest (Mark 2:23–3:6). In these situations, Jesus defended his actions
in two ways: (1) by appealing to precedents in the Hebrew Scripture
and the Prophets and (2) by a more radical appeal that, as the Son of
Man, He was Lord of the Sabbath and everything else.

Jesus had entered Jerusalem on a donkey, an act reflecting that
Jesus was the awaited king described in Zechariah 9 (Mark 11:1–11;
John 12:12–16). He had protested against the practices in the temple
courts, a direct challenge to the leadership's authority over what
Jews saw as the most sacred space on earth (Mark 11:15–18).[1] Such
actions evoked hopes expressed in works like *Psalms of*

---

[1] I treat these texts and others that lead into this scene in *Jesus According to
Scripture* (Grand Rapids: Baker, 2002), 605–23.

*Solomon* 17:26–31, where the hoped for end-time deliverer purges Jerusalem, or an ancient Jewish prayer like the Eighteen Benedictions, where the hope for restored Davidic rule and the restoration of Jerusalem are placed side by side in the fourteenth of these benedictions. These claims of authority had caused the leadership to ask Jesus about the source of His authority, a fair question given they had not authorized Him to act (Mark 11:27–33). These events form a key background as to why Jesus found Himself in front of the Jewish leadership answering if He was seeking to destroy the temple or was claiming to be the Messiah, the Son of the Blessed One.

What is under examination is the extent of Jesus' claims and authority. This scene does not involve a trial in the formal sense.[2] The leadership cannot give a legal verdict that has the force of law in the Roman world. What they are doing is gathering evidence to make a case to Pilate, who can make such a judgment. In our legal world, this is like a legal inquiry or a grand jury investigation where the question is whether Jesus can be charged legally with a crime against the Roman state. The Jewish leadership could bring such a case to Pilate, especially if it came from the high priest whom Pilate had appointed, so this prehistory of tension that Jesus' ministry generated is important to appreciate as Caiaphas steps forward to ask Jesus a crucial question in Mark 14:61: "Are you the Messiah, the Son of the Blessed One?"

Caiaphas, we should bear in mind, didn't mean what a later Christian would mean by "Son." He simply wants to know if Jesus is claiming to be the Messiah who, it had been promised, would deliver Israel from oppression. He was asking, in effect, "Are you the king?" Alluding back to the promises made to David about his dynastic line (2 Sam 7:12–14), Caiaphas's language hearkens back to the idea that, as God's representative, the king is God's son. This image had been applied to all kings of the line.

---

[2] See Darrell L. Bock, *Blasphemy and Exaltation in Judaism: The Charge Against Jesus in Mark 14:53–65* (Grand Rapids: Baker, 2000), originally *Blasphemy and Exaltation in Judaism and the Final Examination of Jesus* (Tübingen: Mohr/Siebeck, 1998). This is a detailed study of this scene and the Jewish background that informs it.

In a context of restoration and a call to renewal for Israel, it also likely points to a messianic expectation. Leaders like Caiaphas had wedded their fate to Rome in the place of messianic and eschatological expectations like those that Jesus appeared to raise. Jesus' counterclaim of such an authority would be all that was needed to bring Him before Pilate. A king whom the Jewish leadership did not recognize, whom Rome did not appoint, was, in their minds, a threat to the *Pax Romana* and a candidate to go before Pilate. Rome appointed the kings of the empire and was responsible for keeping the peace, stopping anyone who claimed any authority that Rome did not give.

Jesus' response triggers a series of core events that stand at the root of what became a major world religion. What did Jesus say and mean? How was His reply perceived by those who rejected it? Jesus' reply is given variously in the Synoptic Gospels. John does not record this examination, so we are only looking at Matthew, Mark, and Luke. I have defended in detail the historicity of this response in a monograph dedicated to this scene.[3]

The core of Jesus' reply to the question "Are you the Messiah?" is yes—but a somewhat qualified yes, as we will see. "I am," said Jesus. "And you will see the Son of Man sitting at the right hand of the Mighty One and coming on the clouds of heaven" (Mark 14:62 NET). That image of sitting at God's right hand comes from Psalm 110:1. The idea of the Son of Man and coming on the clouds refers to Daniel 7:13. As we have seen throughout this book, Jesus fulfilled a plan that was in place hundreds of years earlier when the Psalms and the prophetic works were written. Whereas Mark records Jesus as answering "I am" to the question of whether or not he was the Messiah, Matthew and Luke both focus on the "qualified" nature of Jesus' affirmative response: "You have said yourself" (Matt 26:64 NET); "You say that I am" (Luke 22:70). I take these qualified responses to indicate He responded positively to mean, in effect, "Yes I am the

---

[3] See Darrell L. Bock, *Blasphemy and Exaltation in Judaism and the Final Examination of Jesus* (Tübingen: Mohr/Siebeck, 1998), 184–237, updated in "Blasphemy and the Jewish Examination of Jesus," *BBR* 17 (2007): 53–114, and in a chapter of the same event in Darrell Bock and Robert Webb, eds., *Key Events in the Life of the Historical Jesus* (Tübingen: Mohr/Siebeck, 2009), 589–667.

Messiah, but not quite in the sense that you asked it." Like Mark, both Matthew and Luke record Jesus speaking of the Son of Man sitting at God's right hand (Matthew also speaks of riding the clouds as Mark does). In other words, Jesus elaborates His position by suggesting that God accepts Him as the Son of Man (Jesus' favorite name for Himself) whether the Sanhedrin does or not. Furthermore, He will sit at the right hand of God and judge those who now sit in judgment on Him.

Standing before those who supposedly have religious authority over Him (and all Jews), Jesus says in effect that God is going to show support for Jesus' claims by bringing the Messiah as Son of Man into ruling authority with Him, regardless of a potential crucifixion. Jesus will occupy a regal-executive position in the program of God. The allusion to Psalm 110 ("sitting at the right hand of God") points to a text that has regal overtones. The authority Jesus has, however, should not be understood as a strictly earthly authority. The reference from Daniel 7 to the Son of Man coming with the clouds pictures an authority received directly from God to judge and exercise dominion. Jesus affirms that God will show the Galilean to have a heavenly vindicated authority. The intimation that Jesus will sit in judgment would have been controversial but not nearly as controversial as the idea that Jesus can sit in the presence of God in heaven and can share God's glory and authority. So Jesus answers the question and also makes a prediction with a promise—God will vindicate Him fully regardless of what the leadership is about to do.

Caiaphas is no amateur theologian. He reacts immediately. He tears his robe, indicating in his view that Jesus has uttered blasphemy and is worthy of death. If Jesus had not been who He was claiming to be and if God were not to vindicate Jesus, Caiaphas would have been right. Jesus has supplied the testimony that leads the Jewish leadership to take Him to Pilate for judgment for sedition. They change the religious charge of blasphemy to a political one; Pilate, after all, had no opinion on the religious controversies of the Jews. But if Jesus claims to be "King of the Jews," that is very much the concern of the Roman authorities, who lay claim to the authority to hire and fire all rulers and governors in their dominions. The Jewish leaders "translate" their charge against Jesus out of its religious significance so that Rome would react to Jesus' claim to be king, something Rome would read as a threat to their own authority. Rome held to law and order. They kept the law and made the order!

It is important to keep an eye on the narrative-theological story line coming out of this scene. It is a key element to understanding the early church's preaching about Jesus as well as the debate that ensued as this new movement emerging from within Judaism engaged other Jews. In effect, this scene says that either Jesus is a figure to be exalted by God or else He is guilty of blasphemy. Subsequent events determined by God help us see what is the case.

On the third day, when God emptied Jesus' tomb in resurrection, the vindication Jesus predicted took place. With it came the evidence of where Jesus had gone as a result of God's activity. He had gone to God's right hand to share in God's presence, authority, and glory in heaven. The work of God in salvation became inseparable from the work of Jesus. This connection forms the background for the second passage we wish to consider. We go back yet again to the crucial text of Acts 2: Peter's speech at Pentecost. We focus now on the apostle's appeal to Joel 2 and the coming of God's Spirit.

### Acts 2 Yet Again: Peter's Words at Pentecost

As we have seen before, Acts 2 summarizes a speech by Peter that accompanied the outpouring of God's Spirit on those who had embraced the hope of Jesus and the inauguration of the new covenant brought about by Jesus' death (Acts 2:38–39; Luke 22:20). The risen Christ, you will remember, had told His disciples to wait in Jerusalem for the forthcoming "promise" of the Father that would clothe the disciples with power, enabling them to minister effectively on God's behalf (Luke 24:49). That is an important part of the context of the Pentecost account of Acts 2. The Spirit came as Jesus had promised.

It fell to Peter to explain what the strange events of that day meant. He went further back than Jesus' promise of a few weeks earlier. He went all the way back to the Old Testament prophet Joel (Joel 2:28-32). God had been promising the Spirit for a long time.

And it will be in the last days, God says,
that I will pour out My Spirit on all humanity;
then your sons and your daughters will prophesy,
your young men will see visions,
and your old men will dream dreams.
I will even pour out My Spirit
on My male and female slaves in those days,
and they will prophesy.
I will display wonders in the heaven above
and signs on the earth below:
blood and fire and a cloud of smoke.
The sun will be turned to darkness,
and the moon to blood,
before the great and remarkable day of the LORD comes;
then whoever calls on the name of the LORD will be saved.
(Joel 2:28-32 as cited in Acts 2:17–21)

The last days, Peter claimed, had arrived. God was making good on His promise.

Note what Peter says in Acts 2:21: "Then whoever calls on the name of the Lord will be saved." Any Jew in the audience would have been familiar with that language and would have known what Peter meant by "the name of the Lord"—or would have thought that he or she did. He was talking about YHWH, the God of Israel, God the Father—wasn't he? It is God who saves and who is called upon, right?

By the end of his sermon, however, Peter has rung a few changes on the familiar imagery from Joel. Appealing to Psalm 16, he says of Jesus, "He was not abandoned to the grave, nor did his body see decay" (v. 31 NET). King David, the author of Psalm 16 and the greatest of all Israelite kings, was a great man, but even David was abandoned to the grave and his body decayed. Jesus, Peter claims, was operating at a whole different level.

Peter then invokes Psalm 110:1:

The Lord declared to my Lord:
"Sit at my right hand
until I make your enemies a footstool for your feet"
(Acts 2:34–35 NET)

Sound familiar? This is the text that Jesus quoted to the Sanhedrin before they sent Him off to Pilate. Jesus, Peter insists, is sitting at the right hand of God, just as He claimed He would at His examination by the Jews. As Peter preached it, "Being therefore exalted at the right hand of God, and having received from the Father the promise of the Holy Spirit, he [Jesus] has poured out what you see and hear" (Acts 2:33, author's translation).

There is something very Jewish about the way Peter makes this argument. He applies an ancient Jewish reading technique known as *Gezerah Shewa*. In this technique, the reader of Scripture links together two passages (or a passage and an event) by terms they share. So in Joel 2:28, as cited in Acts 2:17, we have the idea of the Spirit being poured out (*ekcheō*), then in Acts 2:33, we have the verb repeated in a different form (*execheen*). According to Peter, Jesus is pouring out the Spirit that has been given to Him. In verses 34–35 Peter is combining the idea of Psalm 110:1—Jesus' being seated at God's right hand— with what He did when He got there, namely, distribute the Spirit that had been promised as far back as John the Baptist and Joel. Salvation is being mediated through Jesus, who shares God's presence, a place on His throne, and the execution of salvation.

Because of this sequence of connections, Peter is able to say in Acts 2:36 that God has shown Jesus to be Lord and Christ to Israel. You will remember that in Luke 3 John declared that the Messiah would be recognizable by the fact that He would baptize in the Spirit. If Israel wants to know who Jesus is, they can look at what God has done through Him.

There is another complicated *Gezerah Shewa* here, as the term *Lord* (*kyrion*) appears in verse 36, invoking the presence of the second use of the term *Lord* from Psalm 110:1 in verse 34 (*kyriō*), while also recalling verse 22 from Joel 2, where one is to call upon "the Lord" (*kyriou*).[4] The significance of this becomes evident when Peter calls on the crowd to be baptized "in the name of Jesus the Messiah for the forgiveness of your sins" in Acts 2:38. Salvation—including the forgiveness of sins—is now taking

---

[4] It may look like these words are not exactly the same for those who work in English only. However, the forms differ because of the different grammatical role of the word in the two sentences. This involves the difference between an object and a modifier in Greek, which causes the same word to be spelled differently to indicate the difference in its meaning.

place in Jesus' name and by His authority. Peter is equating Jesus, in both His activity and His responsibilities, with the God of Israel. To invoke Him as Lord and Christ is to invoke the authority of God. To call on Jesus' name as Lord is the same as calling on the God of Israel. As Jesus said in John 10:30, "The Father and I are one." In mediating the blessing of God's Spirit, Jesus saves and forgives, undertaking the prerogatives of God and showing divine authority from the very side of God in heaven. Therefore, to call on Him is to call on God. Between the beginning of his speech and its end, Peter has changed the terms of the equation. If his listeners thought they knew what Peter meant by "calling on the name of the Lord," he has given them something else to think about. He is saying that "whoever calls on the name of the Lord will be saved"

One of the great difficulties in sharing Jesus in a Jewish context is explaining how Jesus can receive such unequivocal honor as His believers give Him. Peter's sermon in Acts 2 offers a key to why and how that honor came to be so central to the emerging faith. Here we have Jesus at the hub of divine activity and authority associated with forgiveness and the new covenant. Here the promised Spirit, the sign of the arrival of God's promise for His people, has come. Jesus mediates all of this from God's right hand, sharing in the divine presence, rule, and authority. Everything comes together in what God does through Jesus. Jesus even shares the title of Lord and can be invoked for this salvation because it came through Him, so Peter can speak of God and Jesus in one breath even to the point of sharing a reference in passages that invoke God for salvation.

It is easy to see why Acts 2 is a crucial text for the question we have raised about how Jesus came to be seen as worthy of divine honor alongside the Father. Yet there is one more passage to examine because it appears in what was likely a hymn, showing what first-century Christians were praising God for. It is to this song that we now turn to show that Peter's view was not his alone.

## Philippians 2: A Central Hymn from the Early Church

If Acts 2 helps show us *why* Jesus came to be seen as worthy of divine praise alongside the Father, Philippians 2 helps show what exactly the early church was praising God the Father and God the Son *for*. This passage in Philippians 2 feels quite different from Paul's other writing; the crispness of its contrasts and the balance of its lines suggest that the passage is a hymn—not written by Paul, but quoted by Paul. This origin would mean that it predates the book of Philippians, which was written in the sixties AD. This hymn, therefore, would reflect what Christian communities affirmed as they engaged in corporate praise for what God had done through Jesus, providing a summation of Jesus' career as it was understood at an early point in the theological development of the church.

This hymn speaks of Jesus as the One

> who although he existed in the form of God did not regard
> equality with God as something to be grasped,
> but emptied himself by taking on the form of a slave,
> becoming in the likeness of other men,
> and being found in form as a human.
> He humbled himself,
> by becoming obedient to the point of death—even death on a cross.
> Therefore God exalted him and gave him the name that is above
>     every name,
> so that at the name of Jesus every knee will bow
> —in heaven and on earth and under the earth—
> and every tongue confess that Jesus Christ is Lord
> to the glory of God the Father. (Phil 2:6–11, author's translation)

Much in this hymn is debated. Is its key portrait rooted in a strong sense of the preexistence of Jesus as one sent from heaven, or is it rooted in imagery related to His being the second Adam, a representative of humanity? Is the hymn there to make an ethical point about being like Jesus (because of the call to have a mind like Him), or is it more concerned with Jesus' identity? The career of Jesus is seen as a reverse parabola, which has Him coming and sent from heaven, dipping down to take on humanity and death, only to ascend again to greatness by receiving the name of Lord. All of these important questions about the passage have led to no shortage of opinions. In other words, the literature on this text is vast, but I am not interested in the hymn as a whole or in these specifics debates. Our focus is on how the hymn ends, in verses 10–11.

Because the twin themes of every knee bowing and every tongue confessing have precedent in the Hebrew Scripture, we need a context to get the force of the point. In Isaiah 45:20–25, God is calling all to account for denying the Creator and engaging in idolatry rather than giving God the honor due to Him. So He calls the nations to court:

> Gather together and come! Approach together, you refugees from the nations! Those who carry wooden idols know nothing, those who pray to a god that cannot deliver. Tell me! Present the evidence! Let them consult with one another! Who predicted this in the past? Who announced it beforehand? Was it not I, the Lord? I have no peer, there is no God but me, a God who vindicates and delivers; there is none but me. Turn to me so you can be delivered, all you who live in the earth's remote regions! For I am God, and I have no peer. I solemnly make this oath – what I say is true and reliable: 'Surely every knee will bow to me, every tongue will solemnly affirm; they will say about me, "Yes, the Lord is a powerful deliverer."'" All who are angry at him will cower before him. All the descendants of Israel will be vindicated by the Lord and will boast in him. (Isa 45:20–25, NET)

This text is one of the clearest declarations of God's uniqueness and sovereignty in the Hebrew Bible. God declares that allegiance will be uniquely His one day. There is no other God, nor is there any other savior or judge. Every knee will bow, and every tongue will confess that God is the Lord, a powerful deliverer. The name given above every name is that which affirms the sovereignty of the Creator God over those whom He rules. There is no other place to go. There is no other one to turn to. One day all creation will know and affirm this.

Paul was a rabbi. He surely knows this background as he cites this hymn with its allusion to Isaiah 45. In the Philippian hymn, however, the bowing of the knee and the confessing of the tongue include giving such honor to the Lord Jesus. His work of emptying and death is so conjoined with the Father and so rooted in a heavenly origin that the honor due the God of Israel will come to be given to the One through whom God worked. Once again, we see that substituting Jesus in the place of the God of Israel is kosher, justified by the calling and activity of Jesus at God's behest. Note how the hymn makes clear that God is the one giving Jesus His name and this role. Jesus does not act or claim to act independently of the Father. They are like a double helix in a piece of DNA, a package deal operating as an inseparable team to deliver. They save with a mighty hand that, ironically, stretches out through the death of a frail human who once had been in the presence of God and who afterward was vindicated and returned back to that position. To see and speak of one is inevitably to see and speak of the other.

This kind of identification had always been at the core of the teaching of the early Jesus community. It led later to the technical, philosophical articulation of the relationship between God and Jesus that we see in later creeds. Those creeds seek to translate the appropriate connections we have traced throughout our three passages. They express them in terms of the kind of person Jesus had to be for this role to be the case. Jesus shares such glory without division from the Father.

## The *Shema* Revisited in the New Community

### First Corinthians 8:4–6

Three ideas controlled the affirmation of monotheism in Second Temple Judaism. They were the idea of only worshiping God (monolatry), the idea of God's universal sovereignty, and the idea that God is the one Creator.[5] The early Jesus community affirmed Jesus as divine while affirming the unity of God. Nothing shows this more powerfully than the way Paul plays with the idea of creation and the confession of the *Shema* in 1 Corinthians 8:4–6.

---

[5] These three themes are developed in detail in a series of important essays by Richard Bauckham, *Jesus and the God of Israel: God Crucified and Other Essays on the New Testament's Christology of Divine Identity* (Grand Rapids: Eerdmans, 2008).

Here is the text laid out in parallel structure in English:

> With respect to eating food sacrificed to idols,
> we know that an idol in this world is nothing,
> and that there is no God but one.
> If after all there are so-called gods,
>     whether in heaven or on earth
> (as there are many gods and lords),
> but for us [there is] one God, the Father,
> from whom [are] all things and we for him,
> and one LORD, Jesus Christ,
> through whom [are] all things and we through him. (author's translation)

Remember, Paul made these remarks in the context of the Greco-Roman world, with its many gods. The text affirms the oneness of God in the face of that polytheism. Should any Jew worry that Paul is suggesting that affirming Jesus as divine makes more than one God, this text shows Paul to be resolutely monotheistic. Jesus is God, Lord, Creator, but there is Father and Lord. Paul's language describes who God is and what God does: in Judaism, only God creates (Isa 44:24; 4 Ezra 3:4; Josephus, *Contra Apion* 2.192). And yet, "all things" are created through Jesus—which puts Jesus in the category of Creator, not creature.

Note the connection between Paul's language ("One God . . . One Lord") and the *Shema* ("The Lord [*kyrios*] our God [*ho theos*], the Lord [*kyrios*], is one"). Paul's point is that there is one Father and one Lord who participates in the creation as the Creator. This is all under the heading God with the *Shema* in the background. This affirms a divine activity and status for Jesus as the Christ. Here it is kosher not to substitute Jesus for God but to place Him alongside God to show their equality. Just as we had seen in Jesus' trial before the Sanhedrin, Jesus shares God's glory by His exaltation to God's throne. He also shares the divine task of creating the world as the One through whom the creation of all things took place.

Such a handling of the *Shema* helps us see how Jesus was presented in the earliest Christian community rooted in the writings of believers emerging from Judaism. They did so affirming the oneness of God and the deity of Jesus as Creator and as the

One who sits on the throne of heaven. This final idea of being seated on the lofty throne of heaven depicts Jesus' authority as equal to and alongside God. It results in Jesus being worshiped, a key indication of how early believers saw Him. This final idea is powerfully portrayed in Revelation 4–5. In that well-known passage, all creation turns to worship the Lion, and that Lion turns out to be a Lamb. In the Trinity, God is Father *and* Son *and* Holy Spirit. We turn to worship one, and we see three at work in terms of giving salvation and life. What Revelation 4–5 portrays, 1 Corinthians 8:4–6 affirms.

## Conclusion

We have traversed into great mysteries of the early church by examining one aspect of the sacred Hebrew Scripture in the early years of this new Jewish-rooted movement that came with Jesus. These Jewish believers did not just proclaim Jesus; they explained what they believed. They did it by appealing to the affirming actions of God *and* teaching from their Scripture. The gospel was about what God had done *and* promised. In linking Jesus and substituting Him in places where that Scripture had spoken of the God of Israel, they were expressing a core element of their faith.

God had demonstrated to all the world—both inside Israel and outside—who Jesus was. John the Baptist pointed to it when he spoke of the coming of God's Spirit through Jesus. Jesus pointed to it when he predicted a vindication that expressed itself in a tomb emptied three days after a horrific death. The early church preached it when they substituted Jesus and proclaimed Him as Lord in those very places where the uniqueness of God was affirmed in their Scripture. It all reflected the very activity of Israel's own God, who was affirmed as the Creator and Savior of all life through the invitation God extended through Jesus. Delivering the message this way was explanatory and clarifying. It disclosed the mystery of how God had made the choice and took action to work through Jesus from the earth up to heaven. Through these means, we can begin to grasp Jesus' own uniqueness: He was a one-of-a-kind person who brought God's promised kingdom and was called to be God's anointed. And best of all in the view of the early

Jewish Christians, it was all completely kosher. That Jesus can be given divine honor within His work is also good news. It means that the One who did the work can deliver on what He has promised.

## Questions for Discussion

1. What statement got Jesus crucified, and what does it tell us about Him?
2. What do Psalm 110:1 and Daniel 7:14 tell us about Jesus? What does the Son of Man do?
3. What points about resurrection point to the identity of Christ and the content of the gospel?
4. Why is Jesus uniquely qualified to bring the gospel according to Acts 2 and Philippians 2?
5. Why is the background to Isaiah 45 important in understanding its use in Philippians 2?
6. How does Paul alter the *Shema* in 1 Corinthians 8:4–6?
7. What difference does this theme make for me personally?

# Chapter 6

# Embracing the Gospel: Repentance and Faith

. . . . . . . . . .

A sk ten Christians how we should respond to the gospel, and nine (perhaps all ten) will answer "faith." Ask what faith means, and the answer will be trust or belief. We are to believe God for His promises and place our trust in Him. Each is a good answer but not necessarily the whole answer. Faith is not the only term that the Bible repeatedly uses to describe our proper response to the gospel. Faith, by its very nature, underscores the fact that the gospel is not fundamentally about a transaction but about a sustained relationship. The goal of this chapter is to add depth to our understanding of what faith is. We will look at three terms: *turn*, *repent*, and *faith*. Then we will look at a few texts in which a combination of these terms appears, and hopefully the core of the gospel will become clear. What we see in practical terms is that responding to the gospel is not just a momentary action but the embracing of an attitude of trust and gratitude that connects us to God and moves us to respond to Him. In short, faith is what causes us to love God.

## Turn

*Luke 1: Turning to God*

The first key term we will consider is the term *to turn*. This word highlights the change of direction that comes with the response to the gospel. It is rooted in the Old Testament idea of *shub*, which is the Hebrew word for "repent." It is also illustrated in Luke 1:16–17, which describes the way John the Baptist will set the table for the

89

coming of Jesus: "He will turn many of the people of Israel to the Lord their God. And he will go as forerunner before the Lord in the spirit and power of Elijah, to turn the hearts of the fathers back to their children and the disobedient to the wisdom of the just, to make ready for the Lord a people prepared for him" (NET).

This passage puts John in a long line of prophets. It portrays him as doing what prophets usually did, which was to call people back to God. He will call them *to turn*. But look what happens when people turn: fathers and children will be brought together; the disobedient will return to the wisdom of the just. In other words, there is an ethical dimension to turning back to God: it impacts how we relate to others. When we honor God, reconciliation follows. John prepared a people by opening their hearts up for the change of direction that was to come through Jesus and His message. That change of direction impacted not only how they would see God but also how they would come to regard others.

Consider the movement of the Ten Commandments, from commandments about how we deal with God ("You shall have no other gods before Me," "Remember the Sabbath and keep it holy") to commandments about how we deal with others ("You shall not steal," "You shall not covet"). Something similar is happening here in Luke: the preparation of the gospel focuses first on how people relate to God, and out of that grows a change in the way people relate to others. To turn to God and trust Him is to embrace the example of forgiveness that changes the dynamic of relationships. Applying that forgiveness and graciousness in relationships can lead to reconciliation.

### Short Messages and Summaries in Acts

The book of Acts is often not brought into discussions about the gospel, which is odd because this book is where, more than any other book of the Bible, we see the gospel preached. We have already seen one key text in Acts 2, where Peter calls the nation to repent and respond to the offer of the Spirit that comes with forgiveness of sins. By the same token, in Acts we have ample opportunity to see how people responded to the gospel. Again and again, in both the sermons preached in Acts and the responses of those who hear those sermons, Luke uses the word *turn*. The evangelists call the people to turn, and the people turn—or, as in many cases, choose not to turn.

In Acts 9:35, Peter takes the gospel to Lydda and Sharon. When Peter heals the paralyzed Aeneas, the text says they "saw him and turned to the Lord." In Acts 14:15, Paul urges the people in Lystra and Derbe "that you should turn from these worthless things to the living God, who made the heaven, the earth, the sea, and everything in them." He says this as he is "proclaiming the good news" to them. In Acts 26:18, Paul notes that part of his message entails a call from the Lord "to open their eyes so that they may turn from darkness to light and from the power of Satan to God, that they may receive forgiveness of sins and a share among those who are sanctified by faith in Me."

So we see in these few texts that the proper response to the gospel is *to turn*. When we embrace the gospel, we have undertaken a change in direction. It is a *turning point* that pulls us into and makes us responsive to God's light. We are no longer traveling the road we had been traveling. Oriented differently before, now we trust God and open ourselves up to be directed by Him.

## First Thessalonians 1

In the first chapter of Thessalonians, Paul recaps the way his friends in Thessalonica first received the gospel he preached, commending them for their eager embrace of the truth: "For they themselves report about us what kind of reception we had from you: how you turned to God from idols to serve the living and true God, and to wait for His Son from heaven, whom He raised from the dead—Jesus, who rescues us from the coming wrath" (1 Thess 1:9–10). Once again, the response is summarized in terms of a change of direction. In fact, the issue is stated as a change in loyalty. They turned to God from lifeless idols, and their service was now directed to the true and living God. Paul is drawing on long Judaic tradition here. Those who worship lifeless idols are lifeless themselves unless and until they worship the living God (see Ps 115:4–8 and Isa 44:17–20).

This first chapter of Thessalonians raises another point about the change of direction. It involves a redirection of loyalty. We ally ourselves to God. We also look forward to all that the gospel will bring when the Son returns from heaven to finalize the justice and righteousness He initiated when He died and rose again. To turn is to reorient oneself—including all of one's hopes and desires—to God. It is an act of a moment that changes one's trajectory to and for life.

One need only visit a Greco-Roman city to sense what was involved here. If one goes to Pompeii today, one can walk by a series of temples, each focused on a different god. In this world, one appealed to all the gods to make sure every sphere of life was covered. In addition, family gods, known as *lares*, were worshiped daily in each home. So to embrace a single God for all spheres was not only to change direction but also to totally change one's orientation to life. Believers were called atheists by their Greco-Roman neighbors because they did not believe in the array of gods seen to be at work in the city or home. That change is what 1 Thessalonians affirms as a believing response.

## Repent

### Matthew 3–4

At the start of His ministry, Jesus issued a call to repent. This is where His message about the kingdom began. The call mirrors one John the Baptist made as noted in Matthew 3:2: "Repent, because the kingdom of heaven has come near!" In Matthew 4:17, Jesus echoes that call word for word: "Repent, because the kingdom of heaven has come near!" This term is then picked up in the early church in its preaching. To experience the gospel means to change one's thinking. The point here is very similar to what we have seen with the idea of turning.

### Luke 3

The term *repent* in Greek means "to change one's mind." It assumes that we are open to changing what we have thought about God and about our own relationship with Him. It calls for rethinking the way we relate and respond to God. It also can touch on how we relate to others as a result—that ethical impact I noted when we discussed the mission of John the Baptist and the term *to turn* in Luke 1:16–17. Another text shows us this dimension of repentance. In Luke 3:8–14, a group of people ask John the Baptist what they should do to repent before God. Here is what the prophet says:

> Therefore produce fruit consistent with repentance. And don't start saying to yourselves, "We have Abraham as our father," for I tell you that God is able to raise up children for Abraham from these stones! Even now the ax is ready to strike the root of the trees! Therefore every tree that doesn't produce good fruit will be cut down and thrown into the fire."
>
> "What then should we do?" the crowds were asking him. He replied to them, "The one who has two shirts must share with someone who has none, and the one who has food must do the same."
>
> Tax collectors also came to be baptized, and they asked him, "Teacher, what should we do?" He told them, "Don't collect any more than what you have been authorized."
>
> Some soldiers also questioned him: "What should we do?" He said to them, "Don't take money from anyone by force or false accusation; be satisfied with your wages."

Repentance, because it is a change of mind, entails a willingness to change direction. This text vividly shows this as the crowd asks John what they should do when they "make" repentance. The English obscures the idea of the Greek. John's call to produce fruit worthy of repentance and his hearers' repeated question "What are we to do?" share the same Greek verb *poieō*. This verb means "to do" or "to make something." I note this passage not to say that the gospel requires works but to highlight that John's hearers understood that a change of mind means a willingness to change and be open to what God will do in our relationship with Him. This is because the gospel not only looks back to forgiveness of sins but also looks forward into our new relationship with God.

The application of the point is clear. Repentance is not merely an internal act of the mind; it involves an attitude that results in concrete change of practice. Even the way those in the crowd ask the question about what they should do shows that they understand that repentance shows itself to be present in a resulting change of practice.

*Luke 15*
Jesus affirms the idea of repentance as He defends His initiative to reach out to tax collectors and sinners in Luke 15. In telling the parables of the lost sheep and lost coin, Jesus ends the story with the same refrain: nothing evokes more joy in heaven than the repentance of sinners. That is why God goes out in search of those who are lost, just as the shepherd went looking for his lost sheep and the woman went looking for her lost coin: "I tell you, in the same way, there is joy in the presence of God's angels over one sinner who repents." How are we to respond to the gospel? By changing our minds. By repenting. The desire to see the lost regained motivated Jesus to take the initiative in relating to tax collectors and sinners in a manner that the Pharisees did not. Far from taking any initiative in reaching out to sinners, the Pharisees complained about Jesus' outreach to them, which was why Jesus told these parables in the first place.

The application for our lives is clear. Those who have benefited from and appreciate the gospel are to take the initiative in letting others know about it. If we believe the gospel ourselves, we will desire to seek the lost by taking the initiative to relate to those outside the faith. We will engage them in genuinely pursued relationships. We will be involved in their lives and love them with a love that reflects the values of the gospel, just as Jesus did.

*Luke 24: The Mission According to the Old Testament*
Another lesser-known text comes in Luke 24. The Great Commissions of Matthew 28:18–20 and Acts 1:8 are more famous. Matthew tells the church to make disciples, and Acts 1:8 tells the earliest disciples to await coming of the Spirit before going out into the world with the gospel. The commission in Luke's Gospel makes another point, teaching that the task facing the disciples was rooted in the teaching of Moses, the Prophets, and Psalms. Luke 24:44–49 says it this way:

Then He told them, "These are My words that I spoke to you while I was still with you—that everything written about Me in the worship of Moses, the Prophets, and the Psalms must be fulfilled." Then He opened their minds to understand the Scriptures. He also said to them, "This is what is written: the Messiah would suffer and rise from the dead the third day, and repentance for forgiveness of sins would be proclaimed in His name to all the nations, beginning at Jerusalem. You are witnesses of these things. And look, I am sending you what My Father promised. As for you, stay in the city until you are empowered from on high."

Jesus tells them that the call to take the gospel out into the world was originally made in the Old Testament. This was nothing new. Jesus does not give us any passages here, but the promise made to Abraham that was noted earlier belongs here, as do texts like those Paul cites in Romans 15:8–12.[1] The message is one of "repentance for forgiveness of sins," proclaimed in the name of Jesus. If any text makes it clear that repentance is a proper summary term for the gospel response, it is this passage. Of course, Jesus commissions these disciples because they have seen the events they would preach about and could serve as "witnesses" of Him and those events. However, they were to wait for the Spirit before setting out. The events of Acts 2 and Pentecost that were covered earlier portray this spiritual empowerment. In that passage, the call to repent is also present.

*Summaries and Short Messages in Acts*
Acts 11:15–18 (NET) summarizes Peter's defense of why he welcomed Gentiles as equal to Jews when Cornelius came to the faith.

---

[1] Romans 15:8–12 says, "For I tell you that Christ has become a servant of the circumcised on behalf of God's truth to confirm the promises made to the fathers, and thus the Gentiles glorify God for his mercy. As it is written, 'Because of this I will confess you among the Gentiles, and I will sing praises to your name.' And again it says: 'Rejoice, O Gentiles, with his people.' And again, 'Praise the Lord all you Gentiles, and let all the peoples praise him.'" And again Isaiah says, 'The root of Jesse will come, and the one who rises to rule over the Gentiles, in him will the Gentiles hope'" (NET). The texts cited in Romans 15 in order are Ps 18:49; Deut 32:43; Ps 117:1; and Isa 11:10.

The Spirit was the blessing of the new era, Peter argued, and God had given the Spirit to the Gentiles just as He had to the Jews at Pentecost:

> "Then as I began to speak, the Holy Spirit fell on them just as he did on us at the beginning. And I remembered the word of the Lord, as he used to say, 'John baptized with water, but you will be baptized with the Holy Spirit.' Therefore if God gave them the same gift as he also gave us after believing in the Lord Jesus Christ, who was I to hinder God?" When they heard this, they ceased their objections and praised God, saying, "So then, God has granted the repentance that leads to life even to the Gentiles."

In this explanation, we see many of the things we have stressed throughout this book. We see the promise of the Spirit that, as John the Baptist preached, would indicate the new era brought by the Messiah's arrival. We see the Spirit as the harbinger of restored relationship with God. We also see that repentance leading to life is the proper response of these first Gentiles who came to faith.

In Acts 17:30–31, Paul is preaching at Mars Hill in Athens. In the midst of his message, he describes what God calls on people to do in responding to Jesus. He says, "Therefore, having overlooked the times of ignorance, God now commands all people everywhere to repent, because He has set a day on which He is going to judge the world in righteousness by the Man He has appointed. He has provided proof of this to everyone by raising Him from the dead." Paul points to the accountability all have before God for their lives. Jesus is portrayed as the appointed judge. Acts 10:42 makes a similar point.[2] The need is for a change of mind and in our lives before Him in response.

In Acts 20:20–21, Paul summarizes his preaching mission to the elders at Miletus, saying that when he came to them, he "did not shrink back from proclaiming to you anything that was profitable, or from teaching it to you in public and from house to house.

---

[2] Acts 10:42 says, "He commanded us to preach to the people, and to solemnly testify that He is the One appointed by God to be the Judge of the living and the dead."

I testified to both Jews and Greeks about repentance toward God and faith in our Lord Jesus." Two key terms are used here side by side. We change our minds about God and place our trust in the Lord Jesus. Faith is the intersection of repentance and turning, where mind and action unite.

Sometimes people wish to make a big distinction between faith and repentance, accepting faith as the term for responding to the gospel, while treating repentance as a term that does not have the same kind of theological significance. This passage argues against making such a distinction. What we are seeing is that each of these terms is important. Each highlights a distinct aspect of what is fundamentally one response. In sharing the faith with others, we can speak of turning, repenting or believing as we call people to respond to and believe in God.

Earlier we looked at Acts 26:20, which referred to the idea of turning. In the same context two verses later, Paul speaks of repentance when he says, "I preached to those in Damascus first, and to those in Jerusalem and in all the region of Judea, and to the Gentiles, that they should repent and turn to God, and do works worthy of repentance." Here Paul notes that in preaching the gospel he called for repentance as the proper response. Even more this apostle of grace and salvation by faith alone asked people to turn to God and perform deeds consistent with that repentance. His summary reminds us that the call to faith involves a change of mind, which leads to action. Works emerge as faith's intent. The emerging application to this teaching is important. Faith leads to a way of relating to God that by its very nature leads to a responsive, fruitful life.

## Romans 2

Throughout this book, we have been tracing Paul's presentation of the gospel in Romans. Repentance fits in here as well. In the midst of a section early in this letter, Paul shows how Jews are as subject to God's judgment as Gentiles. He challenges them in regard to God's kindness and where it should lead. So he asks them in verse 4, "Or do you have contempt for the wealth of his kindness, forbearance, and patience, and yet do not know that God's kindness leads you to repentance?" (NET). Repentance, in the end, is not a response growing out of the fear of God's punishment. It is a response to God's abundant kindness, forbearance, and patience. Repentance calls us to change our minds about God. It reflects an attitude that is open to thinking in a fresh way and in new directions. It also leaves us open to think about how we might live differently before God as we ally ourselves with Him and His grace.

## Faith

By far the most common way to summarize the proper response to the gospel is to talk about *faith*. The simple definition of faith is trust. This idea is so fundamental to Christianity that we often refer to Christianity simply as "the faith." Faith is an idea worth probing. For one thing, it is not static. That is, we do not have faith in a moment; it is an ongoing state. This is part of what tells us that the gospel is about more than a transaction. An act of faith initiates our new relationship with God, but faith is not a one-time act; it keeps going. When we equate faith with belief, we are talking about an ongoing faith, not merely a moment of intellectual assent. This is why trust, or reliance, is better a synonym than belief. This faith means that we are open to God and responsive to Him. Without that responsiveness, faith is not faith.

### *Matthew 8 and Luke 7: The Faith of a Centurion*
To illustrate the dynamics of faith, it will be helpful to look at a passage where Jesus commends another for his faith. In fact, this is one of the few passages where Jesus speaks so positively of someone's response to Him. The story of the healing of the centurion's slave appears in two Gospels in slightly different versions. In Matthew 8:5–13, the centurion interacts directly with Jesus. In the parallel of Luke 7:1–10, the interaction takes place between Jesus and Jewish envoys sent on behalf of the centurion. Because this story occupies a similar location in each Gospel and the contents of the story are so similar, we are likely dealing with the same story. It appears that Matthew has simplified the story by removing the envoys and having the centurion interact directly with Jesus; it is the centurion's desires, after all, that drive the

story. Because the teaching on faith is the same in both accounts, I will discuss the Lucan version. Here is the passage:

> When He had concluded all His sayings in the hearing of the people, He entered Capernaum. A centurion's slave, who was highly valued by him, was sick and about to die. When the centurion heard about Jesus, he sent some Jewish elders to him, requesting him to come and save the life of his slave. When they reached Jesus, they pleaded with him earnestly, "He is worthy for you to grant this, because he loves our nation, and has built us a synagogue." Jesus went with them, and when He was not far from the house, the centurion sent friends to tell him, "Lord, don't trouble yourself, since I am not worthy to have you come under my roof. That is why I didn't even consider myself worthy to come to you. But say the word, and my servant will be cured. For I too am a man placed under authority, having soldiers under my command. I say to this one, 'Go!' and he goes; and to another, 'Come!' and he comes, and to my slave, 'Do this!' and he does it." Jesus heard this and was amazed at him, and turning to the crowd following him, He said, "I tell you, I have not found so great a faith even in Israel!" When those who had been sent returned to the house, they found the slave in good health.

What made the centurion's faith so outstanding? There are several features worth noting here. First is the humility of the man. He sees that he is not worthy to invite or presume upon someone like Jesus. Second is how the man understands that Jesus has the kind of authority whereby He only needs to speak to make things happen. Third, he also appreciates that Jesus need not even enter his home to exercise that authority. The man understands that Jesus does not have to be physically present to do His work. There is no sense of entitlement in the centurion (who, in everyday life, would have been entitled to quite a lot), only a deep trust that Jesus is able to do what is asked of Him. This portrait of faith is outstanding because the centurion appreciates the impact and the power of Jesus' authority. He relies on it totally and humbly. Faith in the case of the gospel is a trust that relies on what God has promised through Jesus.

The application here is that faith expresses itself in a way that is obvious in its reliance on Jesus. The centurion's belief expressed itself in a trust that did not require that Jesus respond on the centurion's terms, but he was comfortable allowing Jesus to simply give His word. The word of Jesus was all the centurion needed because he trusted that Jesus' word was effective.

*John 3*

Among passages that highlight faith, John 3:14–18 is probably the best known. Beyond the sometimes comical John 3:16 sign at a sporting event, this passage has been seen as briefly encapsulating the story of the gospel. There is an illustration and then the point:

> Just as Moses lifted up the snake in the wilderness, so the Son of Man must be lifted up, so that everyone who believes in Him will have eternal life.
>
> For God loved the world in this way: He gave His One and Only Son, so that everyone who believes in Him will not perish but have eternal life. For God did not send His Son into the world that He might judge the world, but that the world might be saved through Him. Anyone who believes in Him is not judged, but anyone who does not believe is already judged, because he has not believed in the name of the One and Only Son of God.

Here faith is presented in terms of belief. But it is a belief that acts just as the illustration from Numbers 21:5–9 shows. Jesus' example involves an incident where God judged the people for grumbling but also provided a way out of the judgment if they would look at a bronze snake Moses held up:

> The people spoke against God and Moses: "Why have you led us up from Egypt to die in the wilderness? There is no bread or water, and we detest this wretched food!"
>
> Then the LORD sent poisonous snakes among the people, and they bit them so that many Israelites died. The people then came to Moses and said, "We have sinned by speaking against the LORD and against you. Intercede with the LORD so that He will take the snakes away from us." And Moses interceded for the people.

Then the LORD said to Moses, "Make a snake image and mount it on a pole. When anyone who is bitten looks at it, he will recover." So Moses made a bronze snake and mounted it on a pole. Whenever someone was bitten, and he looked at the bronze snake, he recovered.

Just like the belief that had to be acted on to look at the bronze snake, so to believe Jesus is to trust Him for the deliverance God offers through Him. The passage has more than a mere intellectual assent in view. Relying on someone means to respond to someone and embrace their initiative to act on our behalf. It means entry into a relationship where we respond to God. Later in John 3:36, the point is made this way: "The one who believes in the Son has eternal life, but the one who refuses to believe in the Son will not see life; instead, the wrath of God remains on him." Entry into life is participating in the process of knowing God (John 17:3).

### Other Johannine Summary Statements

The focus on believing that we see in John 3 also appears in several other locations in John's Gospel. In John 5:24, Jesus says, "I assure you: Anyone who hears My word and believes Him who sent Me has eternal life and will not come under judgment but has passed from death to life." In John 6:29, Jesus says, "This is the work of God: that you believe in the One He has sent." Jesus as the commissioned One from God is a key theme in John's Gospel. In fact, John 1:1–18 made clear, as we saw earlier, that the Sent One is God in the flesh.

John 6 is full of summaries invoking belief. In John 6:35, Jesus uses the image of bread as sustenance to picture His work. He declares, "I am the bread of life. . . . No one who comes to Me will ever be hungry, and no one who believes in Me will ever be thirsty again." John 6:40 says it in terms of God's will: "For this is the will of My Father: that everyone who sees the Son and believes in Him may have eternal life, and I will raise him up on the last day." The litany of summaries on believing in Jesus in John 6 ends with this simple summary in verse 47: "I assure you: Anyone who believes has eternal life." The picture of bread is of taking something for sustenance, for maintaining life. Just as we eat meals to maintain life, so we "take in" Jesus to be sustained spiritually.

Yet another important summary is present in John 7:38–39. Here belief in Jesus leads Him to provide beyond the giving of life. The remark comes with an explanation to make it all clear: "The one who believes in Me, as the Scripture has said, will have streams of living water flow from deep within him. He said this about the Spirit, whom those who believed in Him were going to receive, for the Spirit had not yet been received because Jesus had not yet been glorified." Here is the gospel in capsule. Faith yields eternal life and the relationship with God given through His Spirit. This is in conjunction with promises made in Scripture. This image contains an allusion to the new covenant and the picture of being sprinkled clean with the Spirit, all promises we have already discussed. So faith embraces what God graciously gives, making us responsive to the Spirit He gives us to empower and direct us.

John 11:25–26 highlights belief in the context of resurrection. Jesus speaks to Martha as He prepares to bring Lazarus back to life. The verse reads, "Jesus said to her, 'I am the resurrection and the life. The one who believes in Me, even if he dies, will live. Everyone who lives and believes in Me will never die—ever. Do you believe this?'" Notice the repetition: three "believes" in three short sentences.

In John 12:44–46, belief is like a light coming into darkness: "Then Jesus cried out, 'The one who believes in Me believes not in Me, but in Him who sent Me. And the one who sees Me sees Him who sent Me. I have come as a light into the world, so that everyone who believes in Me would not remain in darkness.'" John is using an array of images, each designed to urge people to embrace Jesus and His work in faith. This is why at the end of his Gospel John says he has written his Gospel "so that you may believe Jesus is the Messiah, the Son of God, and by believing you may have life in His name" (John 20:31).

*Summaries in Acts*
Summaries in Acts also make much of faith. Faith summaries are so plentiful in Acts that I will only look at a few. Here is the list of

other verses I will not discuss: Acts 4:4; 5:14; 8:12; 9:42; 13:12; 13:39,48; 16:31; 17:12; 17:34; and 18:8.

A few summaries in Acts are especially significant. We noted Acts 11:17, where Peter speaks of Gentiles being granted repentance and life parallel to what the early disciples received at Pentecost. Belief and repentance are two ways to look at the same appropriate response to the gospel.

In Acts 11:20–21, Cypriot and Cyrenian men took the gospel to Hellenists in Antioch, "proclaiming the good news about the Lord Jesus." Their response is also noted as a summary affirms: "The Lord's hand was with them, and a large number who believed turned to the Lord." Here we have the terms *belief* and *turn* side by side. Again, these terms describe two aspects of the same fundamental response. To believe is to have turned to God from something else.

In Acts 15:8–9, we get another summary of Cornelius's response to Peter's preaching of the gospel. Once again, we get a mixture of images: "And God, who knows the heart, testified to them by giving the Holy Spirit, just as He also did to us. He made no distinction between us and them, cleansing their hearts by faith." Here faith leads into the washing imagery we discussed earlier. Peter also stresses that the Spirit being given is evidence that washing led to a new relationship.

*Romans and Other Pauline Epistles: Faith in Paul's Gospel*
Paul also takes on this emphasis. In a text we referenced earlier, Paul says in Romans 3:21–22, "But now, apart from the law, God's righteousness has been revealed—attested by the Law and the Prophets—that is, God's righteousness through faith in Jesus Christ, to all who believe, since there is no distinction." As Paul argues, the solution to sin's disruption of our relationship with God is to embrace the righteousness God gives through Jesus for both Jew and Gentile without distinction. In Romans 4:24–25, Paul notes that this righteousness is credited to those "who believe in Him who raised Jesus our Lord from the dead. He was delivered up for our trespasses and raised for our justification." Jesus' death pays for sin and His resurrection leads to God declaring us

righteous, so we can be indwelt and be righteous. His new life becomes our new life.

Paul notes the result of this work in Romans 5:1–2 when he summarizes, "Therefore, since we have been declared righteous by faith, we have peace with God through our Lord Jesus Christ. Also through Him, we have obtained access by faith into this grace in which we stand, and we rejoice in the hope of the glory of God." Not only does God view us as innocent, He also is at peace with us. More than that, God gives us access to Him. Faith is the key to our relating to God. We also can look forward with hope to the rest of what God will do when He completes the salvation He started.

All these benefits appear in a confession Paul presents in 10:8–9: "The message is near you, in your mouth and in your heart. This is the message of faith that we proclaim: if you confess with your mouth, 'Jesus is Lord,' and believe in your heart that God raised Him from the dead, you will be saved." Faith says *I understand that Jesus is the One with spiritual authority to deliver and save me.* Faith says *I understand this Lord is alive and I can rely on Him to apply His work on my behalf.* All of these passages on faith show us how faith opens us up to God, making us responsive to Him.

Paul says similar things beyond Romans. In a text we have already treated, Galatians 2:16, Paul makes clear it is faith, not works of the law, that saves: "And we have believed in Christ Jesus, so that we might be justified by faith in Christ and not by the works of the law, because by the works of the law no human being will be justified." Ephesians 2:8–10, the most famous Pauline summary, says that by grace we "are saved through faith, and this is not from yourselves; it is God's gift—not from works, so that no one can boast" (vv. 8–9).

For Paul, faith was a key summary term for a proper response to the gospel. It is God's work that saves us. It is through God's grace that we can turn to Him in faith. However, this faith is not merely an act in a moment; it is an orientation that opens us up to respond to God and be led by Him. It leads us into following His path, because we trust Him (v. 10).

## *James 2: A Faith That Works*

Anyone who has studied James 2:14–26 knows that this key passage has been the subject of much discussion. On the surface James appears to be at odds with the emphasis we have seen on faith elsewhere in the New Testament, but this difference is not as great as many argue. James is dealing with a different question. Unlike the summary passages we have surveyed that present how we get in at the start, James is asking what faith looks like when we look back on it after time has passed. This different temporal perspective argues that faith "works" because its relational reliance and allegiance result in a product:

> What good is it, my brothers, if someone says he has faith, but does not have works? Can his faith save him? If a brother or sister is without clothes and lacks daily food, and one of you says to them, "Go in peace, keep warm, and eat well," but you don't give them what the body needs, what good is it? In the same way faith, if it doesn't have works, is dead by itself.
>
> But someone will say, "You have faith, and I have works." Show me your faith without works, and I will show you faith from my works. You believe that God is one; you do well. The demons also believe—and they shudder.
>
> Foolish man! Are you willing to learn that faith without works is useless? Wasn't Abraham our father justified by works when he offered Isaac his son on the altar? You see that faith was active together with his works, and by works, faith was perfected. So the Scripture was fulfilled that says, Abraham believed God, and it was credited to him for righteousness, and he was called God's friend. You see that a man is justified by works and not by faith alone.
>
> And in the same way, wasn't Rahab the prostitute also justified by works when she received the messengers and sent them out by a different route? For just as the body without the spirit is dead, so also faith without works is dead.

The faith James describes, even though it is faith in God, shows itself in how we treat others. This is the same point that the passages on turning and repentance made, as we saw in the remarks of John the Baptist in Luke 1:16–17 and 3:10–14. However, the key idea is how faith, because of its nature in relying on God, can be counted on for a product. Justification, James says, is by works and not by faith alone. By this he means that faith is completed (or perfected) by works. Real faith has a product. In this way James completes what Paul had already suggested in Ephesians 2:10: "For we are His creation—created in Christ Jesus for good works, which God prepared ahead of time so that we should walk in them." By design, grace leads into works because of a trusting, grateful heart. All of this teaching shows that whether we think of Paul or James, the point of faith is that it is open and responsive to God. Faith is not a mere act taken in a moment; it is a fresh orientation of responsiveness to God.

*First Peter*
Once again, we return to a text we have already referenced. First Peter stresses how faith is an ongoing attitude. Peter notes it in a word of praise in 1:3–5 when he says, "Blessed be the God and Father of our Lord Jesus Christ. According to His great mercy, He has given us a new birth into a living hope through the resurrection of Jesus Christ from the dead, and into an inheritance that is imperishable, uncorrupted, and unfading, kept in heaven for you, who are being protected by God's power through faith for a salvation that is ready to be revealed in the last time." Faith is seen as the dynamic that triggers our protection in the gospel, an idea that is rarely discussed. Faith and God's power stand together as a protection for us as we journey through the gospel experience. So Peter comes alongside Paul and James to make clear that faith is not an act taken alone in a single moment, but a relationship that continues through time.

*First John: Faith as Ongoing*
A nice summary of what God asks of us in the gospel appears in 1 John. John boils down the key two things God asks of His children: "Now this is His command: that we believe in the name of His Son Jesus Christ, and love one another as He commanded us" (3:23). Believing in the name is to believe in a person. It is the relational reliance or allegiance also called faith. The second is an ethical commitment that grows out of such a turning to God—when we

love God, we love the other members of the community. John virtually links the two here and throughout his letter. If we believe in the Son, then we will love the brethren because faith will lead us to be responsive to His command.

We have seen the centrality of faith in the gospel message. It appears throughout those New Testament passages we have already examined, and for good reason: it is connected to all the themes we have been discussing. Faith pulls these themes together because it triggers the entire package of benefits. Faith opens us up to respond to God's work in our lives. We come to Him humbly knowing we need what only He can provide—and He comes through every time. At its core, faith is a humble turning to God in trust. That trust is not present only at the moment of initial belief; it fuels the progress of spiritual life.

## Summary: The Terms Together

In this final section, we briefly look at a few texts where the terms *turn*, *repent*, *faith*, or *believe* occur together. These passages show how interconnected these ideas are.

### Mark 1: Repent and Believe

In Mark 1:15, we see the call of the kingdom summarized with Jesus' words, "The time is fulfilled, and the kingdom of God has come near. Repent and believe in the good news!" People need to be open to change their thinking about God to believe the gospel. That is Jesus' call. Be open to thinking anew about God.

### Acts 3: Repent and Turn

In a speech recorded in Acts 3, Peter explains the power that healed a lame man and issues a call to embrace the gospel, which combines some of our terms: "Therefore repent and turn back, that your sins may be wiped out so that seasons of refreshing may come from the presence of the Lord, and He may send Jesus, who has been appointed Messiah for you. Heaven must welcome Him until the times of the restoration of all things, which God spoke about by the mouth of His holy prophets from the beginning" (vv. 19–21). Thinking anew about God and turning back to Him lead to the removal of sin, which gives new life. This also ushers us into a program wherein one day Jesus will return to make all things right, an event this text calls a restoration. This faith also extends into the future, looking to what God has yet to do and knowing that these promises also will come to pass.

*Two Pauline Summaries from Acts:*
*Faith, Turning, Repentance*

Two texts in Acts juxtapose our terms through the teaching of Paul. We considered Acts 20:21 earlier in the chapter, but it is important to look at it here as well because it juxtaposes faith and repentance in ways that show how one relates closely to the other: "I testified to both Jews and Greeks about repentance toward God and faith in our Lord Jesus." If we change our minds about God and trust Jesus, then we experience all the benefits that a relationship with God offers. Because there are many ideas about God in our world, just as there were in the time of the apostles, we have to change our thinking about God and about ourselves to be in a position to trust in Jesus. By nature, we would prefer to trust in ourselves, but we need to move away from such a view, which cuts us off from God's provision. This openness or repentance makes us willing to think anew about God and Jesus.

The result of repentance is what makes it such an important term in this discussion alongside faith. Repentance allows us to recalibrate how we view God and receive what He wishes to give us. God seeks to empower us, but He does not force it down our throats; He desires that we seek it.

In Acts 26:15–23, we get the fullest summary of Paul's view of the gospel and his own mission as he received it from Jesus:

> "But I said, 'Who are You, Lord?'
>
> "And the Lord replied: 'I am Jesus, whom you are persecuting. But get up and stand on your feet. For I have appeared to you for this purpose, to appoint you as a servant and a witness of things you have seen and of things in which I will appear to you. I will rescue you from the people and from the Gentiles, to whom I now send you, to open their eyes that they may turn from darkness to light and from the power of Satan to God, that they may receive

forgiveness of sins and a share among those who are sanctified by faith in Me.'

"Therefore, King Agrippa, I was not disobedient to the heavenly vision. Instead, I preached to those in Damascus first, and to those in Jerusalem and in all the region of Judea, and to the Gentiles, that they should repent and turn to God, and do works worthy of repentance. For this reason the Jews seized me in the temple complex and were trying to kill me.

Since I have obtained help that comes from God, to this day I stand and testify to both small and great, saying nothing else than what the prophets and Moses said would take place—that the Messiah must suffer, and that as the first to rise from the dead, He would proclaim light to our people and to the Gentiles."

In this text, all our key terms appear: *repenting, turning,* and *faith.* Paul stresses how this message grew out of a program God designed and revealed in Scripture, namely, that the Messiah would suffer and rise from the dead so that light could be proclaimed both to Jews and Gentiles. God not only showed who Jesus was; He revealed the program beforehand. What Paul presents here is Jesus' own outline of the gospel. In the end, it is an opportunity to change our minds about God, turn, and trust Him, believing in the work and authority of our deliverance from sin by Jesus. This brings us into a new relationship with God through His Spirit. It is good news that this gift is available to all. Its successful execution is the work of God, and we can trust God to do what He had set out to do long ago. But God does not force it on us. So repenting, turning, and faith are three parts of a single triangle of response. Repenting looks at where we start. We change our mind about God. Turning pictures the process of the change of direction. Faith is where we end up. We are trusting in God and His provision of life in the Spirit through Jesus. Having changed our minds about how we see Him and ourselves, He calls us to faith— which is a turning and an embracing. The openness of faith means we embrace what God offers. The good news is we do not earn it; we simply receive it as the gift it is designed to be.

## Questions for Discussion

1. Define what turning, repentance, and faith mean.
2. Is each of these terms useful in discussing the response to the gospel? Why?
3. What is the relationship of the three terms to each other in thinking through responding to the gospel?
4. What do responses in Acts stress?
5. What does Paul stress in responding to the gospel?
6. What does James stress in responding to the gospel?
7. Why is faith called relational reliance in this chapter? Which New Testament scene most powerfully pictures it?
8. What do John's epistles and Peter's letters stress?
9. What difference does this theme make for me personally?

# Chapter 7

# A Different Kind of Power Through a Way of Life Pleasing to God: Reconciliation, Peace, and Power of God unto Salvation

· · · · · · · · ·

Our world likes power—talking about it, gaining it, wielding it. Power is about control. Power, we believe, lets us control others, our environment, our circumstances. Many are attracted to the powerful, no matter how they use that power. It is their aura of control that is appealing.

The gospel is also about power—but a power used in a completely different way from the way the world sees it. That is our focus in this chapter. In this chapter, we are more interested in the impact and the results of the gospel than its content. In this impact lies much of the practical hope of the good news for our world. We will look at three key results of the gospel at work in human lives: reconciliation, peace, and power.

## Reconciliation

*Romans 5: From Separated to Reconciled*

Paul is one of our key sources for understanding the gospel. In Romans, he lays his views out most systematically. Roman 5:1–11 is a good place to start looking at Paul's vision for reconciliation. We have already looked at the beginning of this text, which speaks of our access to God in a restored relationship through the gospel.

Here we consider what comes with that relationship and the results of the gospel:

> Therefore, since we have been declared righteous by faith, we have peace with God through our Lord Jesus Christ. Also through Him, we have obtained access by faith into this grace in which we stand, and we rejoice in the hope of the glory of God. And not only that, but we also rejoice in our afflictions, because we know that affliction produces endurance, endurance produces proven character, and proven character produces hope. This hope does not disappoint, because God's love has been poured out in our hearts through the Holy Spirit who was given to us.
>
> For while we were still helpless, at the appointed moment, Christ died for the ungodly. For rarely will someone die for a just person—though for a good person perhaps someone might even dare to die. But God proves His own love for us in that while we were still sinners Christ died for us! Much more then, since we have now been declared righteous by His blood, we will be saved through Him from wrath. For if, while we were enemies, we were reconciled to God through the death of His Son, then how much more, having been reconciled, will we be saved by His life! And not only that, but we also rejoice in God through our Lord Jesus Christ, through whom we have now received reconciliation.

Several things result from the gospel according to this passage: peace, access, character, hope, and to top it all off, reconciliation. We have gone from separated to reconciled. Reconciliation looks at two parties previously at odds and now brought back together. Whether we think of peace treaties, estranged family members, or a separated couple who comes back together, reconciliation is always a special moment. Such a turn of events is a cause for rejoicing. It is not surprising, then, that Paul speaks of how this salvation yields reconciliation and leads to joy.

We should not miss how we get here. It is in Christ's work for us while we were yet sinners. This reconciliation is distinct from many other forms. In a typical reconciliation, two or more parties have to meet in the middle. Here the initiative belongs strictly to what God has done through Jesus. God reconciles us through the death of His Son, who died for us while we were yet sinners—which is to say, when we were unable to have grabbed onto God, He reached out to us. God undertook this sacrifice even though we did not deserve it. Yet God's love and commitment to bring us back to Himself extended this far. Here is yet another description of God's grace touching us at His instigation. Out of this reconciliation come peace, access, character building, and hope.

Often people like to preach the gospel as if it will bring well-being or prosperity. It does bring these things but not necessarily in the manner the theme is often preached. The gospel promises a well-being that is based on character that emerges stronger because of the access and reconciliation God gives. It produces a character that can work through hard times. The prosperity that comes is the prosperity of the soul, not a guarantee of material wealth. It is one of the great distortions of the gospel to suggest that it brings health and wealth in a material sense. The gospel moves beyond this to spiritual well-being. Take a moment and read through Romans 1–8; there is nothing about material prosperity to be found. It's all about spiritual well-being, even in circumstances that could cause us to groan. Reconciliation puts us back into God's hands, and that helps us negotiate the waves of life.

*Second Corinthians 5 and Acts 17:*
*Ambassadors with a Message of Reconciliation*
In many ways, the idea that we are ambassadors with a message of reconciliation stands behind why I wrote this book. Paul gives disciples their marching orders here in terms of their tone as they present the gospel. When I spoke in an earlier chapter of Jimmy Cagney theology and a message that says, "You dirty rat, you should not be doing that," I had in mind a tone that does not fit the good news we have surveyed together. In this short passage pointing to reconciliation, we see the tone Paul desires we have as ambassadors who represent God in the world:

> Now everything is from God, who reconciled us to Himself through Christ and gave us the ministry of reconciliation: that is, in Christ, God was reconciling the world to Himself, not

counting their trespasses against them, and He has committed the message of reconciliation to us. Therefore, we are ambassadors for Christ; certain that God is appealing through us, we plead on Christ's behalf, "Be reconciled to God." (2 Cor 5:18-20)

We have a calling to be God's ambassadors in the world. We are now foreigners representing a different kingdom and loyalty. We also have a message that this world is not all there is to life. Our message is in a sense very much a plea. That plea is "be reconciled to God." He cares for you, and separated from Him, you are not making the most of your life. You could have and experience so much more. The tone here is very much one of invitation and consideration. Paul did challenge with accountability, but he did so also with a tone of appealing to people to be reconciled to God.

We see this tone in a fascinating passage in Acts 17:16–32. Paul is in Athens. The text tells us that He is angry at all the idols He sees there. In fact, if we wish to have a sense of how Paul feels about this kind of rejection of God, we need only read the opening verses of Romans 1:18–23.[1] Yet when he addressed the Athenians, he did it respectfully even as he challenged them to think differently about God. He invited them to consider how they are accountable to God. He did not finish his message because when he got to resurrection, discussion ensued. Nevertheless, the passage shows Paul preaching as an ambassador giving an invitation to think afresh about God. He is calling for repentance even as he seeks faith:

---

[1] Romans 1:18–23 says, "For God's wrath is revealed from heaven against all godlessness and unrighteousness of people who by their unrighteousness suppress the truth, since what can be known about God is evident among them, because God has shown it to them. From the creation of the world His invisible attributes, that is, His eternal power and divine nature, have been clearly seen, being understood through what He has made. As a result, people are without excuse. For though they knew God, they did not glorify Him as God or show gratitude. Instead, their thinking became nonsense, and their senseless minds were darkened. Claiming to be wise, they became fools and exchanged the glory of the immortal God for images resembling mortal man, birds, four-footed animals, and reptiles."

While Paul was waiting for them in Athens, his spirit was troubled within him when he saw that the city was full of idols. So he reasoned in the synagogue with the Jews and with those who worshiped God, and in the marketplace every day with those who happened to be there. Then also, some of the Epicurean and Stoic philosophers argued with him. Some said, "What is this pseudo-intellectual trying to say?" Others replied, "He seems to be a preacher of foreign deities"—because he was telling the good news about Jesus and the resurrection.

They took him and brought him to the Areopagus, and said, "May we learn about this new teaching you're speaking of? For what you say sounds strange to us, and we want to know what these ideas mean." Now all the Athenians and the foreigners residing there spent their time on nothing else but telling or hearing something new.

Then Paul stood in the middle of the Areopagus and said, "Men of Athens! I see that you are extremely religious in every respect. For as I was passing through and observing the objects of your worship, I even found an altar on which was inscribed:

TO AN UNKNOWN GOD

Therefore, what you worship in ignorance, this I proclaim to you. The God who made the world and everything in it—He is Lord of heaven and earth and does not live in shrines made by hands. Neither is He served by human hands, as though He needed anything, since He Himself gives everyone life and breath and all things. From one man He has made every nation of men to live all over the earth and has determined their appointed times and the boundaries of where they live, so that they might seek God, and perhaps they might reach out and find Him, though He is not far from each one of us. For in Him we live and move and exist, as even some of your own poets have said, 'For we are also His offspring.' Being God's offspring, then, we shouldn't think that the divine nature is like gold or silver or stone, an image fashioned by human art and imagination.

"Therefore, having overlooked the times of ignorance, God now commands all people everywhere to repent, because He has set a day on which He is going to judge the world in righteousness by the Man He has appointed. He has provided proof of this to everyone by raising Him from the dead."

When they heard about resurrection of the dead, some began to ridicule him. But others said, "We will hear you about this again."

Do you see the respect Paul gives to the misdirected spiritual quest? He recognizes and seeks to engage them at the level of their desire to know and seek God. Even though that direction is currently misguided, Paul steers them toward what God is doing in Jesus. He pleads with them to be reconciled to the living God, all the while beginning to make it clear they are accountable to Him.

Paul can do this in part because in the ancient world there was a healthy respect for God. People did not debate whether there was divinity in the world. Some of that is not a given today. Some people feel they can barter with God and that He owes them. Or they have a view of God that sees Him more like a grandfather who can be manipulated rather than as the sovereign Lord. Nevertheless, the point is that we need to offer the gospel with a tone of invitation even as we challenge people to think afresh about how they see God. Our job is not to seal the deal or press people; it is to present the message of hope. The results are in the hands of those who listen to us and the God who can work to change a person's heart.

This issue of tone is so important. The church often loses its way here. It either sugar coats the gospel so much that the need (and resultant gratitude that comes from having that need met) is lost or it wags a finger in someone's face trying to shame him or her into the kingdom. Neither of these approaches is what Paul shows us here. Respect those on a spiritual quest. Invite them to be reconciled to God and to sense their need for what He has done. Then be content to leave the results of that conversation in the hands of those who are invited and the God who does the inviting through you. Remember that the gospel comes with its own power as the Word of God. Its hope can penetrate the heart in ways we never can as the Spirit of God goes to work in seed that gets planted through the sharing of that positive message.

## Peace

A goal of the work of Jesus as the Messiah is peace. This note is struck in one of Luke's opening hymns when Zechariah pictures the One to Come as the morning dawn bringing light to darkness.

Luke 1:78–79 says, "Because of our God's merciful compassion, the Dawn from on high will visit us to shine on those who live in darkness and the shadow of death, to guide our feet into the way of peace."

### Romans 8: Peace in the Spirit

The key role of the Spirit in the new life is a central idea of the gospel. Paul ends his journey through the gospel story with a look at this theme in Romans 8. In this chapter, Paul is clear that the Spirit—that giver of life and peace—is indispensable to the gospel:

> What the law could not do since it was limited by the flesh, God did. He condemned sin in the flesh by sending His own Son in flesh like ours under sin's domain, and as a sin offering, in order that the law's requirement would be accomplished in us who do not walk according to the flesh but according to the Spirit. For those whose lives are according to the flesh think about the things of the flesh, but those whose lives are according to the Spirit, about the things of the Spirit. For the mind-set of the flesh is death, but the mind-set of the Spirit is life and peace. For the mind-set of the flesh is hostile to God because it does not submit itself to God's law, for it is unable to do so. Those whose lives are in the flesh are unable to please God. You, however, are not in the flesh, but in the Spirit, since the Spirit of God lives in you. But if anyone does not have the Spirit of Christ, he does not belong to Him. (8:3-9)

For Paul the dynamic that drives the new life is the Spirit of God. All believers have this gift dwelling within them. This empowerment is what changes us. The Spirit is the mark that we belong to God.

Two things mark the presence of the Spirit—life and peace. By "life," Paul means a way of living that honors God. The peace Paul refers to involves relating to God with no barrier between Him and us thanks to the work of Jesus Christ. The Spirit's presence means we have peace with God. This idea is reinforced by what Paul says in Romans 14:17 as a kind of summary: "For the kingdom of God is not eating and drinking, but righteousness, peace, and joy in the Holy Spirit."

When we are in Christ, we pursue this reconfigured life in a fellowship with God that has Him on an open line. His Spirit within prompts us. Our involvement with His community encourages us. This does not mean that the Christian life is trouble-free—far from it. What it does mean is that our identity is clearly established, as is our allegiance to Him. This pulls us in a positive direction with a new possibility for living that we did not have before God entered into our lives. Relationship with God pushes us to pursue God even more.

### *Ephesians 2: Reconciled to One Another in Peace*

Besides peace with God, there is a relational peace that comes with the gospel. This point is made clear in a long and developed text in Ephesians 2:11–22, where Paul highlights how Gentiles moved from being distant from God's promise to being equal partners with the Jews, who originally had received the hope of messianic deliverance. More than that, the result was a new kind of peace found in a newly formed community, what Paul called the one new man, or humanity, Jesus had formed:

> So then, remember that at one time you were Gentiles in the flesh—called "the uncircumcised" by those called "the circumcised," done by hand in the flesh. At that time you were without the Messiah, excluded from the citizenship of Israel, and foreigners to the covenants of the promise, with no hope and without God in the world.
>
> But now in Christ Jesus, you who were far away have been brought near by the blood of the Messiah. For He is our peace, who made both groups one and tore down the dividing wall of hostility. In His flesh, He did away with the law of the commandments in regulations, so that He might create in Himself one new man from the two, resulting in peace. He did this so that He might reconcile both to God in one body through the cross and put the hostility to death by it. When Christ came, He proclaimed the good news of peace to you who were far away and peace to those who were near. For through Him we both have access by one Spirit to the Father.

So then you are no longer foreigners and strangers, but fellow citizens with the saints, and members of God's household, built on the foundation of the apostles and prophets, with Christ Jesus Himself as the cornerstone.

The whole building is being fitted together in Him and is growing into a holy sanctuary in the LORD, in whom you also are being built together for God's dwelling in the Spirit.

Jesus has formed a new institution, where Jews and Gentiles both have access to God and share in reconciliation with each other. Paul calls this message to which they responded the good news of peace, dealing not only with individuals' relationship to God but also with how they associate with each other. As fellow citizens of a kingdom and fellow family members, they share a sacred place—"a holy temple" according to Paul—where God dwells with them. The link that joins them together is God's Spirit. The gospel extends out to change our human relationships as well as the way we relate to God.

The application is a new set of renewed relationships that comes alongside an individual relationship to God. In this new community, we find encouragement, hope, and examples of others who have taken this path to life. No Christian is called to be an island. Reconciliation allows us to be sure we are part of a team.

### Colossians 3, 2 Timothy 2, Hebrews 12, and 2 Peter 3: Called to Peace in the Body of the Messiah

Paul again speaks of peace in Colossians, where he speaks of our calling. The short final exhortation in 3:15 is as simple as it is profound. He says, "And let the peace of the Messiah, to which you were also called in one body, control your hearts." In the context, Paul has discussed the clothes of virtue a Christian is to wear: "Therefore, God's chosen ones, holy and loved, put on heartfelt compassion, kindness, humility, gentleness, and patience, accepting one another and forgiving one another if anyone has a complaint against another. Just as the Lord has forgiven you, so also you must forgive. Above all, put on love— the perfect bond of unity" (Col 3:12–14). This peace has a relational dimension to it. With it, we are now equipped for a better quality of relationship with others; we can be compassionate, kind, humble, gentle, patient, accepting, and forgiving. It's a recipe for good relationships.

This relational peace is something we are to seek, as 2 Timothy 2:22 teaches: "Flee from youthful passions, and pursue righteousness, faith, love, and peace, along with those who call on the Lord from a pure heart." Hebrews 12:14 says something similar when it exhorts, "Pursue peace with everyone, and holiness—without it no one will see the Lord." So also 2 Peter 3:14 says, "Therefore, dear friends, while you wait for these things, make every effort to be found in peace without spot or blemish before Him."

This string of texts from different writers shows that the pursuit of peace is an important calling of those who have experienced the peace that comes from God. The gospel that yields peace with God calls us to be at peace with others. Our security in Him facilitates peace with others. The peace clears the path to be part of a new community of fellow travelers on this journey with God. Like mariners navigating a ship through unpredictable seas, the people of the new community keep us in touch with the power and peace of God, allowing us to see our way clear.

## The Power of God

In many ways looking at the power of God sums up all that we have said about the gospel. In fact, this summary term is the one Paul applies to the gospel in a central text found in Romans 1.

### Romans 1: The Gospel as the Power of God

In Romans 1:16–17, there is a text that I had read for years without appreciating its key point. These verses are well known as they appear in almost any Scripture memory program for new believers. The text reads, "For I am not ashamed of the gospel, because it is God's power for salvation to everyone who believes, first to the Jew, and also to the Greek. For in it God's righteousness is revealed from faith to faith, just as it is written: The righteous will live by faith." I read this passage for years, focusing on the gospel as being about the salvation of God, which it certainly is; however, the gospel is more than a transaction and delivery.

When I realized that Paul was talking about the gospel as power, I also realized that the gospel extended far beyond a mere transaction. The part of the gospel that was transaction opened up a new vista of connection with God, making me aware of provision I had hardly explored. The fact that God enables meant the pressure was off of me to perform or engender my own spiritual experience; rather when I turned to God and engaged His power, He was now free to work through me as I gave Him my spirit to work in conjunction with His Spirit. From that surrender emanates a satisfaction about life and a set of values that connected me in new ways to creation. The result was satisfaction about living and a sense of real purpose in life, yielding both a new kind of dedication and a new kind of peace.

So the summary word Paul picked to discuss the gospel and explain why he values it is *power*. For a long time I had no idea why this word was here, and then it dawned on me that these verses introduce us to the entire account of Romans. These verses are like an opening aria in an opera where we hear the key musical themes summarized in anticipation of the rest of the story. Then my mind walked through Romans. First, it discusses how man is trapped in sin, helpless (read *powerless*) to escape the dilemma in which he finds himself. Then in 3:20–5:21, we have the justification God brings through Jesus. In chapters 6–8, we see the sanctification that comes through the Spirit. The key idea in these final chapters is that we are now capable of living in a way both as individuals and as a community that honors God after being completely powerless before the Spirit came into our lives. That Spirit came when we responded to the gospel with faith and gained access into the new relationship it provided. What had Paul excited about the gospel was this new, vibrant relationship that came with the Spirit of God. That is the story of Romans. That is the gospel he wanted the church in Rome to appreciate. That is the good news we have sought to recover in this book. It is good news to know that God gives us the power to live as He designed us to live. That power stands at the center of the gospel. The church needs to rediscover this truth of the gospel and draw upon it for the power to live as God originally intended.

Here is the grand point in all we have said. The good news is that God indwells us to show us we are His children. His Spirit enables us to be His children and to live like it. In all of this, our purpose for living finds a home as the image of God in us comes to more healthy expression. In a very real sense, we reconnect with ourselves at a level far deeper (read *as we were created to be*) than we could have imagined before the lines were reinstated. The ultimate good news of the gospel is that in finding and knowing God, we come to truly find and know ourselves. But we only get there by participating in that new life and drawing on the resources God has given us. Those resources are the Spirit within and the rooted-in-God community we share with others around us who also appreciate the journey. To embrace the gospel is to embrace not only a rediscovered God of grace but also a new way of living and a new family. The gospel is never about me; rather, it is about God and His restoration of creation. Life with God becomes an eternal journey of discovery, and thanks to the work of Christ, we are able to share in it. Perhaps the best news of all is that when the good news becomes our story, our life is forever changed and deepened in ways we otherwise could not have anticipated.

## Questions for Discussion

1. Why is power associated with the gospel, and what kind of power is it?
2. What is the relationship of reconciliation to the gospel? How do we concretely show reconciliation in a way that points to and affirms the gospel by the way we live?
3. How does Paul's presentation of the gospel in Acts 17 show the gospel as good news? How does the tone differ from Romans 1, and why is that difference important to understand and apply?
4. What dimensions of peace does the gospel bring? Is it only peace between an individual and God? How do we show

this fruit concretely in a world that needs to hear and see the gospel?

5. How important are corporate relationships to the outworking of the gospel?

6. How important is it to the church to show the gospel in giving evidence of reconciliation, works of compassion, and service as well as to share that message verbally?

7. What difference does this theme make for me personally?

# Conclusion

# Getting the Gospel Clear: A Relationship Rooted in God's Love, Not Just a Transaction

* * * * * * * * *

The gospel is not about a business deal. It is rooted in something far more profound—God's pursuit of us in relationship as He restores creation to its intended design. I want to summarize what we have done by focusing on some points that indicate God's motivation in offering the gospel. This also is good news because it shows God seeking to engage us at the deepest levels of our being and to motivate us for that engagement. In a sense, the question is, Why should God pursue those who have chosen to go their own way? It may seem odd to end our study here, but this topic allows us both to review key points and refocus on the rationale that motivates those whose story becomes intertwined with the gospel. There are two parts to the answer of why God pursued us when we turned from Him: first, God loved us; second, God sought to motivate us through His love.

## The Gospel and the Love of God

There are several passages to consider, and although we could easily expand the list, we will only note a few of these texts.

*Portraits of God's Love from John*
John 3:16 reads, "For God loved the world in this way: He gave His One and Only Son, so that everyone who believes in Him will not

perish but have eternal life." God's love for humanity motivated Him to design the gospel as a work He achieved through His Son. The text focuses on love as the motivation and the bringing of life as the goal.

When we hear the words *eternal life*, we think of its duration. This is life without an end. That is part of the point. However, the definition of this term later on in John's Gospel gives it an additional important dimension. In John 17:3, as Jesus utters a final prayer before His arrest and death, He says, "This is eternal life: that they may know You, the only true God, and the One You have sent—Jesus Christ." Eternal life is about not only its duration but its source, the eternal Creator who can give that life as the author of it. To live eternally is to be lifted out of this temporal, temporary world and into the presence of God. To know Him and the One sent from Him is to enter into life without end, just as Jesus had promised in John 4:10–14 to the Samaritan woman when He said,

> "If you knew the gift of God, and who is saying to you, 'Give Me a drink,' you would ask Him, and He would give you living water."
>
> "Sir," said the woman, "You don't even have a bucket, and the well is deep. So where do you get this 'living water'? You aren't greater than our father Jacob, are you? He gave us the well and drank from it himself, as did his sons and livestock."
>
> Jesus said, "Everyone who drinks from this water will get thirsty again. But whoever drinks from the water that I will give him will never get thirsty again—ever! In fact, the water I will give him will become a well of water springing up within him for eternal life."

What motivated Jesus? He wanted to offer us life. All we are asked to do is take it as we embrace Him and what He offers.

I often say to my students that living forever is not automatically a great thing. It depends with whom you are spending eternity! There are some scenarios where being around forever could be a nightmare. But to live with someone who loves us—someone who has shown His love through the ultimate sacrifice—assures us that He will care for us even in the midst of the hardest times. It is reassuring to know that God acts out of His desire to draw near to us.

*Romans 5: God's Love According to Paul*
Romans 5:8 is not complex: "But God proves His own love for us in that while we were still sinners Christ died for us!" The emphasis is on God's initiative. When Jesus undertook the sacrifice, He did so willingly and with love as His forethought.

*Galatians 2: Love as Motivation*
In Galatians 2:19b–20, Paul makes clear what motivates him in his new life with Christ. It is what Christ has done for Him: "I have been crucified with Christ; and I no longer live, but Christ lives in me. The life I now live in the flesh, I live by faith in the Son of God, who loved me and gave Himself for me." This is an echo of what John said about Jesus in John 3. Only here we see that this love of Jesus motivates Paul to draw on and be faithful to the life the apostle received as a gift from God. Here love begets love. Love in turn begets loyalty, which is why faith could be called a type of trust that yields relational loyalty.

*Romans 8: Love as an Inseparable Bond*
There is an important attribute to God's love: It sticks with us. If God can design a plan that reaches out to us even as we seek to walk away, it also can keep us in His grip. Paul knows this as well and concludes his survey of the gospel in one of the most beloved passages in Scripture, Romans 8:35–39:

> Who can separate us from the love of Christ? Can affliction or anguish or persecution or famine or nakedness or danger or sword?
> As it is written: Because of You we are being put to death all day long;
> we are counted as sheep to be slaughtered. No, in all these things we are more than victorious through Him who loved us.
> For I am persuaded that neither death nor life,
> nor angels nor rulers,
> nor things present, nor things to come, nor powers,
> nor height, nor depth, nor any other created thing
> will have the power to separate us from the love of God that is in Christ Jesus our Lord!

Here is the depth of God's love. Nothing can get in its way. The gift of life now bestowed seals us into a bond with God that permits nothing to get in His way. In other words, faith bonds us to God's love, and God's love bonds to our faith. In looking to Him, we have our life. There is nothing left to earn and no need to persuade God of our righteousness. He has given us all the love and support we need. Legalism is ruled out, and a graciousness that naturally seeks to please God steps in. We are willing to do anything for the One we know gave us real life, saving us from the paths of self-destruction in the process. With God fully committed to us, we can be fully committed to Him.

*First John 4: God's Love Begets Our Love*
The apostle John wrote a letter that exhorts us to love. To do so is to reflect the great new commandment Jesus gave to His disciples at the Last Supper. In John 13:34, Jesus says, "I give you a new commandment: love one another. Just as I have loved you, you must also love one another." I bet if we were to ask John what motivates this love, he would tell us to read 1 John. The story we have been tracing about the gospel is the key. First John 4:19 summarizes it this way: "We love because He first loved us." Our love, rooted in the appreciation that comes with our faith, emerges as a response to God and His forgiveness.

## Two Illustrations of God's Love
## and the Response It Engenders

In Jesus' ministry, there are two important texts that describe how Jesus reached out and related to sinners as well as how they responded to Him. We close with these two key illustrative texts.

*Luke 15: Why God Gave the Gospel*
*for Those Who Need It (i.e., All of Us)*
One of the most profound chapters in the New Testament is Luke 15, where Jesus tells three parables about regaining that which has been lost. The passage tells us that He told these stories because some were complaining that He was associating with tax collectors and sinners. Earlier in Luke 5, when a similar complaint had

been registered, Jesus said in verse 31, "The healthy don't need a doctor, but the sick do. I have not come to call the righteous, but sinners to repentance." Jesus was on a mission to heal.

In Luke 15, Jesus tells three stories, one about a lost sheep, another about a lost coin, and a third about a father who embraces a returning and repentant son. In the first two cases, Jesus notes that when we recover what has been lost, there is joy at the recovery, which is how heaven rejoices at regaining a lost sinner. The parables show the effort to regain the lost sheep and coin as a picture of God's initiative in seeking out the sinner. Here is God's love at work.

The last parable I wish to focus on is different. Here we see the reaction of the Father:

He also said: "A man had two sons. The younger of them said to his father, 'Father, give me the share of the estate I have coming to me.' So he distributed the assets to them.

Not many days later, the younger son gathered together all he had and traveled to a distant country, where he squandered his estate in foolish living. After he had spent everything, a severe famine struck that country, and he had nothing. Then he went to work for one of the citizens of that country, who sent him into his fields to feed pigs. He longed to eat his fill from the carob pods the pigs were eating, but no one would give him any. When he came to his senses, he said, 'How many of my father's hired hands have more than enough food, and here I am dying of hunger! I'll get up, go to my father, and say to him, "Father, I have sinned against heaven and in your sight. I'm no longer worthy to be called your son. Make me like one of your hired hands."'

"So he got up and went to his father. But while the son was still a long way off, his father saw him and was filled with compassion. He ran, threw his arms around his neck, and kissed him.

"The son said to him, 'Father, I have sinned against heaven and in your sight. I'm no longer worthy to be called your son.'

"But the father told his slaves, 'Quick! Bring out the best robe and put it on him; put a ring on his finger and sandals on his feet. Then bring the fattened calf and slaughter it, and let's celebrate with a feast, because this son of mine was dead and is alive again; he was lost and is found!' So they began to celebrate." (Luke 15:11–24)

This is how God receives us back when we return to Him. He receives us back fully. This parable is known as the Prodigal Son, but it is misnamed. It really is about the Compassionate Father. His reaction to the son is the heart of the story. Some interpreters want to say that the returning son does not depict repentance. He is just coming back out of a pragmatic desire to have food. I think this misses a very important detail in the story. When the son returns, he makes a confession and seeks not to return as a son but merely as a slave. He knows his previous actions were wrong and is willing to have a demoted status to pay for it. That response pictures someone who turns to God in repentant faith, relying only on the goodwill of the Father, knowing he is not entitled to anything.

The reaction of the Father is just as important to notice. The Father never lets the returning son finish his request. He interrupts before the son asks to be accepted as a slave and receives him back in full as a son. That is a picture of God's forgiveness and His willingness to receive back those who turn to Him and embrace His forgiveness. Here is the tone of the recovered lost gospel— one of rediscovery. God is on a quest to regain us, not to scold us, though He will hold us accountable for ignoring Him. This quest is rooted in the initiating love of God—with His arms extended to receive us back if we will turn to Him. He will not force us to Him. In that genuine response comes the bond that leads to faith, love, and life. Real love genuinely appreciated engenders love in return. This relational dynamic drives the faith and love of the believer. It is this dynamic that fuels responsiveness to God. This dynamic explains how Jesus could teach that the way to eternal life was to love God with all our being. Faith in God means entry into His love that causes us to love and respond to Him in return.

*Luke 7: Jesus Receives an Anointing from*
*a Sinful Woman and Explains Her Love*
One of the most famous of the stories about Jesus comes from a dinner scene where a sinful woman anoints Jesus' feet to the shock of his dinner host. The parable He tells says everything about this passage:

Then one of the Pharisees invited Him to eat with him. He entered the Pharisee's house and reclined at the table. And a woman in the town who was a sinner found out that Jesus was reclining at the table in the Pharisee's house. She brought an alabaster flask of fragrant oil and stood behind Him at His feet, weeping, and began to wash His feet with her tears. She wiped His feet with the hair of her head, kissing them and anointing them with the fragrant oil.

When the Pharisee who had invited Him saw this, he said to himself, "This man, if He were a prophet, would know who and what kind of woman this is who is touching Him—she's a sinner!"

Jesus replied to him, "Simon, I have something to say to you."

"Teacher," he said, "say it."

"A creditor had two debtors. One owed 500 denarii [about two-and-a-half years' wage], and the other 50 [about two-and-a-half months' wage].

Since they could not pay it back, he graciously forgave them both. So, which of them will love him more?"

Simon answered, "I suppose the one he forgave more."

"You have judged correctly," He told him. Turning to the woman, He said to Simon, "Do you see this woman? I entered your house; you gave Me no water for My feet, but she, with her tears, has washed My feet and wiped them with her hair. You gave Me no kiss, but she hasn't stopped kissing My feet since I came in. You didn't anoint My head with oil, but she has anointed My feet with fragrant oil. Therefore I tell you, her many sins have been forgiven; that's why she loved much. But the one who is forgiven little, loves little."

Then He said to her, "Your sins are forgiven."

Those who were at the table with Him began to say among themselves, "Who is this man who even forgives sins?"

And He said to the woman, "Your faith has saved you. Go in peace." (Luke 7:36–50)

This text has many points, but we focus on two that come from the parable in the middle of the story. First, Jesus makes clear that the woman's faith, which He commends as saving her here, is a response to the initiative that God undertook to forgive sin. God's offer of forgiveness, which she appreciated and accepted, motivated her action. Second, Jesus says something very profound here. He says that the depth of our sense of forgiveness will generate an equally deep sense of gratitude. To the extent we think we are entitled to blessing from God, we will demand it from Him and not love Him in response. To the extent we appreciate His grace extended to us when we did not deserve it, we will love Him with a depth of response in appreciation for what God has done.

I love this passage. It flows with God's acceptance and love for those who will turn to Him. I tell a modern version of Jesus' story to illustrate it. Imagine you have a mortgage that you cannot pay. The lender calls and says, "We need to have a talk."

So you go into the lender. He asks where the payments are, and you tell him you cannot pay. His response is that the institution will have to do something about this lack of response. You know what is coming. You are about to lose your house.

Only the lender does something surprising. He reaches into his desk and begins to write. He hands you the mortgage and a check. He tells you to take the check and give it to the clerk to cash it. He has just paid your mortgage. You are free to go with the house now fully yours. Undeserved, your debt is paid. Now if that happened, I bet you'd be grateful to that lender. In fact, I bet you'd be willing to tell others about your great lender.

That is the grace of God in the gospel we have been describing.

The reality of what God is offering is even more powerful than my illustration. We are invited to sit at the table in God's house with His love, power, and protection surrounding us. That offer of new life and relationship with God is the gospel. That relationship, rooted in God's love and everlasting in duration, is what Christianity is all about. That gospel is what the church is called to preach—and to live. It is a message we need to recover and share with a tone that reflects the love and reconciliation that motivates it because it is a testimony to the wonderful and deep love of God for us. Embrace it in faith and share it with others. It is a story of good news worth telling. You never know. Maybe by telling the story, you will end up recovering more than the gospel.

## Questions for Discussion

1. Why is it crucial to see the gospel as more than a transaction?
2. Define eternal life as presented in John 17:3.
3. According to 1 John 4, what is the gospel to produce?
4. Should we take the initiative in engaging with the gospel according to Luke 15?
5. What lesson did the sinful woman who anointed Jesus' feet understand profoundly?
6. Why compare the gospel to sitting at a meal? How relational is the gospel? How relational and engaged should I be with others in order to show and share the gospel? How should the way we share the gospel reflect the heart of God as portrayed to the prodigal?
7. Why is the tone of the church as important as the message of the church when it comes to sharing and communicating the gospel?
8. What difference does this theme make for me personally?

# Appendix:

# Showing the Gospel

· · · · · · · · ·

In this work, I have not developed one very critical question that is a part of many treatments of the gospel. It is the question of how the church shows the gospel corporately by its activity in the world. This is sometimes introduced by speaking of a whole gospel or by saying that we have a hole in the gospel if we do not ask how the church engages as part of its corporate testimony in the world. I have not attempted to address that question in this book directly, as it is a topic all its own. My choice not to discuss this matter, however, is not an indication that I do not believe the topic to be important. It is, but it deserves more than what I am focused on covering here. One can hardly introduce this key topic without getting into some details, but that is precisely what I hope to do in this short affirmation.

Scripture teaches that the Church models its gospel message and commitment to showing God's love for people by the way it engages in service and care in the world. We are to be salt and light, and being salt and light includes caring for and about God's creatures and His creation. There is no reason to have an either-or mentality about these matters: there's no reason to choose between preaching the Word of the gospel on the one hand and serving on the other. That kind of dichotomized thinking is not biblical.

In fact, Jesus preached the Word but also modeled God's love by His care for others, His willingness to heal and show compassion. Word and work were side-by-side, reinforcing one another. Just consider how Jesus preached God's gospel call to the poor and then went in Capernaum and ministered to such people (Luke 4:16–44). One visible expression of care pictured and symbolized

God's deeper love for people. The church not only preached God's love but showed it. One of the most powerful ways the church can build credibility for its message and tone is to demonstrate the love God has for people. Such concern is at the core of Jesus' Sermon on the Mount. When the church shows reconciliation and models it, as well as preaching it as a product of the gospel, it shows what it preaches. The congruence lends credibility to the core message of the gospel that God loves the people He created. I often ask, "When we evangelize, how do we show that we believe our message?" Nothing shows it as powerfully as when our actions reinforce our message.

It is odd that what we do instinctively on the mission field we hesitate to do at home. Part of what created this division is the impact of living in the shadow of a social gospel that lost its roots in the work of Jesus for the inner well-being of people. However, an overreaction the other way is not balanced. This inconsistency is seen, for example, when we readily open a hospital to care for those whom we also share with overseas, yet hesitant to endorse such activity in our own neighborhoods (even though the origins of many of our hospitals at home were in churches sponsoring their creations before there was a social gospel concern). How many of our local hospitals bear the name of a denomination? Ever ask why and what motivated it?

The dissonance of doing one thing overseas and another at home is obvious to many. It is much better to be consistent in preaching the gospel and showing we believe it by how we engage and serve in our communities. Showing the care of what it means to live in light of the good news and in response to it can be as effective a means of revealing God's gospel as speaking about it. It is always best when our words and practice match, so what we say we also show. Such action technically speaking is not the gospel, but such action is necessary to testify to the gospel and testify to its transforming power. For when the Spirit brings new life, the Spirit also brings a new way in living and caring.

# About the Author

Darrell L. Bock is Research Professor of New Testament Studies at Dallas Theological Seminary, as well as Professor of Spiritual Development and Culture. He has written over twenty books ranging from full commentaries on Luke and Acts to specialized academic monographs about Jesus. He also has written opinion page pieces for numerous publications, and he has been interviewed on *ABC News*; NBC's *Today Show*, *NBC Nightly News*, and *Dateline*; ABC's *Good Morning America* and *20/20*; CNN's *Anderson Cooper 360*, *The O'Reilly Factor*, *Mad Money*, *Scarborough Country*, and *CNN Daytime*; Ted Koppel's special *The Lost Tomb of Jesus: A Critical Look*; *NPR News*; the BBC; and the Australian Broadcasting Company. His book *Breaking the Da Vinci Code* made the *New York Times*' best-seller list in nonfiction in 2004. He is an editor-at-large for *Christianity Today* and a past president of the Evangelical Theological Society (2000–2001). He has been married to his wife, Sally, for over thirty years and has three grown children and two grandchildren. This book grows out of his life's commitment to engaging culture concerning issues tied to the gospel and Jesus.

# Name and Subject Index

# Scripture Index

# Apocrypha